Live to be different and to make a difference.

Whenever you find yourself on the side of the majority,

it is time to pause and reflect - Mark Twain

NOVELS BY JOSEPH T.RIACH

The Boy From Broughty Ferry

Too Early For A Glass Of Wine?

and

* Coming Soon – New Mystery Thriller *

INSPIRATIONS

The Secret World Of Self-Employment

Mastering The Art Of Making Money

Self-Improvement Should Be Fun!

Winning Big In Life And Business

The Simplest Sales Strategy

The Road To Joyful Living!

Because I Feel Like It

Yes You Can!

All available in Paperback and E-Book formats at Amazon (.com and .co.uk), Barnes & Noble and all leading bookstores.

More about the author at www.tomriach.com

WINNING BIG IN LIFE AND BUSINESS

Joseph T.Riach

ISBN : 978-1798926628

© Joseph T.Riach 1998–2019 all rights reserved

Joseph T.Riach

CONTENTS

Introduction

Yes You Can! - In Life
How to dare to be different

Yes You Can! - In Business
How to own your own future

Yes You Can - Absolutely Free!
How to win big at zero cost

Conclusion

Joseph T.Riach

INTRODUCTION

ABOUT THE AUTHOR

Joseph Tom Riach was born and brought up in the Scottish city of Aberdeen and educated at its famous Grammar School, as indeed was Lord Byron in a previous era.

A both precocious and introvert child, Tom was an obsessive footballer and sports follower and experienced no difficulty in finding his way into trouble. He once set fire to the family home while lighting a camp fire in the sitting room.

He also liked to write.

Tom particularly dislikes small talk and large groups and would rather listen and think than speak, and write rather than talk. He rarely answers the phone.

In young adult life Tom's passion and drive saw him quickly become self-employed and he excelled as a business consultant and investment adviser. As a serial entrepreneur, he established, acquired and operated several small businesses.

Today he hosts his 'Wake Up Leisure and Learning Breaks', personal mentoring and business guidance, in the calm and tranquility of the sunny south of Portugal.

He also indulges his passion for writing. Tom is the author of several best selling books in the self-help, business, finance and successful living genres.

He is not entrusted with the lighting of fires nor the management of weekend barbecues.

ABOUT THIS BOOK

As a lifelong entrepreneur, as soon as life has looked secure, predictable or straightforward, I have hopped off to one side lured by whatever it is that I've never done before. So, when it is said that within every person there is a book waiting to get out, in my case read several books waiting to get out!

In reality of course very few texts ever escape the realms of the individual's mind and find their way into print. It takes a great deal of time and energy to transform ideas and experiences into a manuscript. The writer must possess the firm conviction that what he has to say will not only be of interest to readers but will capture their imagination and deliver a compelling read.

That 'Winning Big In Life And Business' is the fourth in my current series of writings to appear in print says much about the exotic kaleidoscope of experiences with which my life has been liberally peppered and which have coloured my ideas and perspectives.

I never sought sense, neither indeed wisdom. The crumbs of each which have come my way were delivered rather than ordered. I am constantly and pleasantly surprised to be reminded that even the most bizarre events of my existence are what have primed my pen. Without them there would be no story to tell, no sagacity nor circumspection to pass on.

Just when I think that my bank of personal knowledge has

been well and truly plundered and I think to rest my pen, into my head pops another batch of unlikely and long overlooked experiences. I have used some of these personal stories and anecdotes from time to time in this book, both for the purpose of illustrating certain points and for your entertainment. However improbable (and life does tend to throw up the sublime and ridiculous) all are real occurrences.

Of course, without the many characters who touched my life, be it briefly or more deeply, and brought to it their experiences and influences there'd be no story to tell. My thanks go to every single person mentioned in these pages, however grand and meaningful their contribution or however fleeting. Even more so my thanks go to the considerably greater number of people not mentioned, whoever you are.

All have contributed to my over-riding message of 'Yes You Can!' which is that for all the diversity that exists in defining success, whether a millionaire business mogul or a lone round the world yachtsman or a single parent struggling to make ends meet or one excelling in any area of life or commerce, all successful beings possess two common traits.

The first of these is the quality of perseverance! Persistence and determination alone are omnipotent.

The second is that these super achievers approach, plan and enact their endeavours in a manner totally different from everyone else.

They are contrarians. They dare to be different. They own their own futures.

FOREWORD

We live in a time when free thought and free speech are becoming ever more suppressed; a time when headline electronic chatter seems to be the only form of 'discussion' and the sole source of personal opinions for many and when the expectation of society is that everyone should be equal in mediocrity.

Yet this mass move towards mindless sameness creates fabulous opportunities for those of you prepared to defy the new convention, contradict popular opinion, work things out for yourselves and express yourselves without restraint.

Of course there really is nothing new in this at all. It is just such independent thinkers who have always been at the forefront of all developments in society in every era. It is innovators and contrarians who shape the future and those of you who take control of your own destiny ultimately shape, not only your own lives, but the lives of all.

Once you dare to be different and claim ownership of your own future then winning big in your life and business affairs becomes not only attainable - but a virtual certainty.

Joseph T.Riach

BOOK 1

YES YOU CAN! - IN LIFE

How To Dare To Be Different

Joseph T.Riach

Chapter 1

DARE TO BE DIFFERENT

Only when you dare to be different from others and stand out as one who does not conform to expected norms in the conduct of your life can you expect to achieve great things. There is no other way.

It matters not what your ambitions may be – personal growth, professional advancement, spiritual enlightenment – each or all demand that you pursue avenues of thought and action contrary to those being followed by your peers and society at large. You must become a contrarian.

Sure, there are those who live their lives happy and content in the mediocrity of 'normality', many blissfully unaware that they could be someone or some thing better. But for those of you with a restless spirit, one telling you that you are worth more than just being average and who long to be a -

* *More effective*
* *More efficient*
* *More humane*
* *More caring*
* *More loved*
* *More admired*
* *More content*
* *More relaxed*

- person and feel happy, calm and more in control of your own destiny than is the case at present then you are going to have to behave quite differently from everyone else.

So who or what is a contrarian?

Does it mean that when everyone else turns left, you turn right? When all others say 'Yes', you say 'No'? Not quite ... but ... it does mean that you must be prepared to defy convention and follow your own instincts; those gut feelings with which you were endowed as a primitive being and which still lurk inside you although repressed and sanitised by modern culture.

POWER POINT - *"Summon up the courage to defy convention and follow your own instincts and gut feelings."*

Yet these instincts served your ancestors well and are still fully operational within you, they just need to be released. In order to do that you must remove the clutter clogging their healthy function. You must remove from your very core the negative thoughts, negative people and negative behaviours, many of which have been instilled in you since birth and others which surround you persistently in modern life. To do this takes courage. But steel your resolve. Ask yourself -

Are you prepared to accept a life in which it is other people's suppositions that determine what you feel, think, say and do each day?

and

Why would you accept a valuation of you by society which falls far short of what you know your own self worth to be and your expectation of what you deserve from life?

The answers to both of those questions should be the same resounding - "I will not accept that!" So don't. Determine to experience in life all the exhilaration and joy which is your birthright.

Exercise your freedom of choice to think, say and do the things you want to do, where and when you want and in the manner that you want. Don't be deflected from your course.

Dare to be different!

Chapter 2

A LESSON IN HUMILITY

Life as I know it started with a sharp lesson in humility. It was administered by my mother in the year of my tenth Christmas. She succeeded in her objective admirably!

As a little boy I yearned for all those things which most lads of my age and era longed for. A racing bike (or any bike), a real leather football and a semi-nude photo of Brigitte Bardot! (the last of which frequently changed hands in the school yard for a bag of toffees). But, much as Brigitte's charms tempted me, I more than anything lusted after a Hornby 00 gauge (one hundredth actual size) electric train set!

To own one of these would not only have realised my most fantastic dream but would have raised me to god-like status among my school mates, only one of whom already possessed a version of the treasured toy.

Actually the train set was much more than a toy. It was a precision crafted model to love, cherish and operate like a real engineer, not just play with. The locomotives were exact replicas of legendary British steam engines. The two most famous of which were the Flying Scotsman (the magnificently restored original locomotive runs special tours throughout the UK to this day) and the Mallard. The latter boasted aerodynamic plating in garter blue and is still holder of the world steam loco speed record of one hundred and twenty-six miles per hour. My preference was to have the replica of the Mallard, but either would have done.

Then, on what was to become that infamous Christmas, there below the Christmas tree, beautifully wrapped in red tinsel appeared a package containing one of them! But which one I was never to know.

On the Sunday before Christmas it was customary for all of the children who attended Sunday school at the local presbyterian church to bring with them a present to be placed under the Christmas tree by the altar for later distribution to the poor children of the town. That morning, having been thoroughly scrubbed behind the ears and dressed in my smartest school blazer, grey flannel shorts and brogues polished almost to the point of extinction, my mum took me aside and asked me which of the presents for me under our Christmas tree was my favourite.

I knew pretty well what all the presents were – the shape of the oranges, apples and bananas which most of the roughly wrapped packages contained being easy giveaways – and the train set was the only very large and impressive parcel amongst them. It was also the only one bearing a card proclaiming it be be from my 'rich uncle' in London. Without suspecting for a second the trap set for me, I blurted out, "The electric train of course!"

"Fine," responded mum with not a trace of emotion in her voice or sign of it in her eyes, "Then that's the one that you will take to church for the poor kids." Poor kids! What about me? At that moment I felt as flattened as I would have been if felled by the church bell plummeting from the belfry. My head was ringing, my senses numbed. I was speechless. The tears wouldn't come until later. Then there'd be tears on top of the tears from the beating I received for crying and not caring about the poor kids!

So my train set went on the not unimpressive pile of gifts for the 'poor kids' under the church Christmas tree and I had to sit through a hellfire and brimstone sermon preached at full throttle by the Reverand MacIlwraith about the spirit of Christmas giving.

To make matters worse he stared directly at me and appeared to refer to me specifically as he ranted on about mean spirited sinners who would roast in hell for eternity. At that moment the only people deserving of having their souls warmed down under as far as I was concerned were McIlwraith himself, my mum and the supposedly poor wretch whose ownership of 'my' train set made him, as far as I could see, a considerably wealthier sod than yours truly!

As a result of this chastening experience I grew up in a state of some confusion as to what actually constitutes charity and what is self worth? For my mum and the church clearly considered those poor kids more worthy than me of owning an electric train set. Yet the good reverand himself and the church elders (those members of high standing in the community and appointed to assist the minister in his pastoral and practical duties), appeared to me to enjoy considerable material wealth in their lives. This conflicted with my notion of what the church, and my mum, were instilling in my young mind about the over-riding importance of humility, giving and of spiritual wealth.

To this day I'd say that spiritual well-being starts with

feeling good about yourself and valuing yourself as at least equal to any other person. You must not put yourself, or allow others to put you, on a lower rung of life than that which you merit. Helping others and serving them is fine, it will raise your self-esteem ... but not when done from a begrudging mindset or a belief that your only worth is to subject yourself to the drudgery of being subserviant to others and to their needs.

To this day I resent my mother's action although I have long since forgiven her. I've no doubt that she acted in good faith although most folks to whom I've related this tale over the years agree that she was overly harsh. But yes, I did learn from it.

I learned a lesson in humility, one which has stood me in good stead in many areas of my life. I came to know the lesson of being charitable, caring for others and giving. And, while I learned that it is more meaningful to give something of real value, I also realised that I had to give willingly in order to get something from the experience too.

POWER POINT - *"Generosity should flow from the heart and be enriching to both donor and recipient."*

I also grew up very angry. An anger which hurt many people over the years and most of all hurt myself. This anger stemmed from a feeling of low self-esteem on my part, instilled in part by instances such as the electric train set Christmas present fiasco. It manifested itself as passive-aggressive behaviour on my part, that state of mind whereby you give the impression of going along with what's going on while inwardly resolving not to and then aggressively reacting when challenged about your duplicity.

This feature of having your inward thinking at odds with your outward behaviour is deceptive of course to yourself as much as to anyone else. One of the hallmarks of genuine people, those with a good sense of self-worth and a well balanced view of themselves and of what's going on in life and around them, is that their actions are in line with what they say and what they say is consistent with what they feel. So be honest with yourself.

POWER POINT - *"Say what you feel and do what you say."*

Are you in harmony with yourself and the world around you? Think about it. When the persona you display to the outside world (that's your emotions, words, deeds and actions) differs from the promptings of your inner spirit, you will never be content or at ease with yourself. It's a difficult balance to achieve but one that you should strive for because it is critical to your well-being.

When you see someone confident, relaxed and self-assured, content and enjoying life then it's highly likely that what you're experiencing of their outward self is a mirror of their inner tranquility. But those who display negativity, anger and criticism are at war with their deep inner self, their conscience and their inherent knowledge of what constitutes right and wrong. Their outward behaviour reveals their inner struggle. Such people will mostly blame others for their shortcomings and in doing so continue their downward spiral into ever deeper self-loathing.

There is a way out for these desperate souls, it's not easy. It means -

* Swallowing pride and asking for help

and

* Accepting that the help you need is not the help you had in mind when you asked for it!

This because real help does not come as a quick fix remedy or as a handout. It comes as insistence that you face up to your shortcomings and as encouragement to help yourself by changing yourself (albeit with the tools and instructions as to how to use them provided).

Does this ring a bell? - (not the church one), it should. Because as a free spirit you may believe that you are self-reliant. Yes you are and so you should be. But you also need to be open to help along the way too.

You may think that might mean getting a cash loan from a relative, overdraft facility from the bank or other similar material assistance. But I'd suggest not. No, the help you need is by way of knowledge and training in life skills, being in possession of the right 'tools' and mindset and knowing how to use them.

With those in place you can help yourself to scale the heights of achievement. You can put yourself on an upward spiral from whatever point on 'the scale of life' that you presently occupy. When in the ascendancy your inner spirit will grow and your outward persona will more and more reflect a self-assured and contented being. One truly in harmony with yourself and the world around you.

Count your blessings and realise how valuable you are and how much you have going for you. Move forward to the life that is your birthright with grace, strength, courage, and confidence.

Once thus in harmony with yourself then the world in general will see you as someone to know, like and trust. In this state you can be both humble and generous. You can also fully embrace and enjoy, without misplaced sense of guilt, all of life's riches and the many blessings of both spiritual and material wealth – including ownership of an electric train set!

Chapter 3

DEAD HORSE WISDOM

Y*ou know, you know you never know 'til a dead horse kicks you ...* is just one from the extensive repertoire of oft repeated mottos with which my Uncle Charlie would regale me while on epic walks together around the city of our birth. To him you see had fallen the task of providing respite to my beleaguered parents by relieving them of the young and exhausting me for a few hours on Sunday afternoons. So each week I happily trekked along with him through every close and alley, along every street and avenue and through every area - rich, poor, residential, industrial - of the town, totally absorbed in his constant stories and revelations of the place and those who inhabited it.

My uncle was neither an educated man nor a sophisticated one. He had left school at age twelve and thereafter worked all his days – or rather nights and early mornings – in my grandfather's bakery; but he had a kind heart, native wit and local knowledge fit to confound even the most learned of local scholars and historians.

So much so in fact that I, in later life, would regularly amaze friends and colleagues, and myself too, with impromptu nuggets of information about the city, little known sites and local facts and tales of long forgotten characters who had walked the streets and played out the mosaic of their lives there. I had unwittingly received a complete alternative education from my 'uneducated' uncle!

POWER POINT - *"Never underestimate the wisdom and wit of the common man."*

Another of his favourite sayings which I most enjoyed and which left its indelible mark on me is …

Paddy on the railway breaking up stones, When along came an engine and broke Paddy's bones, "Oh," said Paddy, "That's not fair!" "Oh," said the engine driver, "You shouldn't have been there!"

… What marvelous wisdom to be taught at that young age, more so when viewed against today's irresponsible and blame averse culture.

As a result, I grew up always aware that I, and I alone, was responsible for my life and for all that happened in it. I've survived many scrapes and self-inflicted woes over the years and received my fair share of kicks from dead horses too. Enough to know that the greatest life lesson of all is to know that you never know until you've been kicked by one!

Chapter 4

THE ROAR OF THE CROWD

Did you ever as a child compete against yourself at games when there were no other kids around to play with? Or indulge in solitary practice of a sport but with an imaginary opponent or target involved? And when you 'won' did you acknowledge the roar of a non-existent crowd? If yes then your imagination was serving you well and also preparing you to cope with adult situations that demand solitude.

Self-improvement, for example, is a purely personal thing. Therefore it is not necessary to share it. In fact it's not at all desireable to share it. Apart from the simple fact that it is private, very private, there are two other reasons to keep it to yourself.

One is that sharing with others what you are doing can undo the goodness of your intention. It turns your work on yourself more into a *'look at me'* and *'how good am I'* activity rather than the intimate inner endeavour which it should be.

Secondly, if you do share or if others discover what it is you are about, you will inevitably invite in the critics, doubters and naysayers with their plethora of negative comments and energy sapping ridiculing of your work. So keep your intents to yourself.

Should it happen that others become aware of the fact that you are working to become a better person and they deride what it is that you are trying to achieve then you must not allow the negative vibes with which they bombard you to get to you. You must not allow their mindless envy (for that is what it is) to penetrate your cloak of determination. Rather deflect their negative energy and throw it back on them by adopting an inner "I'll show them!" attitude.

Even if others do not know of or ridicule your efforts it can be a good motivator anyway to create an imaginary foe, someone to compete against in order to strengthen your resolve ... even if, as is the case, the opponent is simply yourself!

In this case you can use "I'll show them!" as a mantra to repeat continuously, both to yourself inwardly and said out loud several times each day.

Such competition with your make-believe adversary can help drive you to new highs, get the crowd roaring - and boy what a kick you get when you give him a real good whopping!

Chapter 5

STRIVING FOR EXCELLENCE

There is little doubt in my mind that the continual striving for excellence in all aspects of my life in which I indulge was instilled in me by my parents from an early age. This conditioning was further reinforced through my formal education and in the many social clubs, societies, sports and outdoor activities in which I participated. Every moment of every day was a blur of activity and in all that I did I was encouraged to be, and often succeeded in being, the best.

This training has done nothing but benefit me throughout my life, I am grateful for the discipline and diligence instilled in me. And yet, whatever my successes and regardless of how many people were impressed, I came to realise that I could never please my mum! For some unexplained reason, which to this day I've failed to uncover, mum could never acknowledge achievements of either myself or my siblings. More bizarre still, she'd wax lyrical and at length about the successes of anybody and everybody else, especially complete strangers!

Johnny so and so, *"the son of the next door neighbour's best friend's second husband's cousin's cleaning woman's auntie"* (get the picture)? would overnight become her endless subject of admiration for having done well at school, won some prize, been promoted at work or for simply existing;

although she had no idea who the guy was other than that she'd heard through the gossip vine how fantastic he was. Yet for me, her own son – never a word of praise, nothing.

One morning (in my adulthood) when I met her for coffee she was reading the local newspaper in which I was featured with accompanying photograph for having won a business award. Throughout the ensuing thirty minutes she made no mention of my achievement, neither did I. Only as I crossed the room to leave did she call after me, "That isn't you in the paper is it?" I threw a look over my shoulder and replied, "No." It's the nearest I ever came to a, "Well done," from her. The words I craved to hear.

I can only say that her attitude caused me to strive ever harder to gain her approval. If a deliberate ploy on her behalf to drive me to continuously greater heights, then she succeeded admirably. To this day, long after her departure from life, I still find myself pushing to do a little better, then a little better again … all perhaps in the hope of eventually pleasing her and gaining her approval.

Then again, I know now that I am in life imperfect, as was my mum before me. She was doing the best that she knew how to and taught me to alway try to be the best that I can be. At the end of the day that's the most that anyone can expect from me and it's the most that I can expect of myself.

And it's the most my mum could ever expect too.

POWER POINT - *"Striving each day to be the best that you can be is the best that you can be!"*

Chapter 6

STRIDING TO VICTORY

When you think of your personal expectations of yourself, your aim should be to be your best self and then just a little better each day. Improvement is simple if carried out in small stages but the cumulative effect over time can be massive.

If a 1500 metre runner has an average stride of one metre then he will take fifteen hundred strides in the course of a race. Were he to add just 5 centimetres to each stride he would reduce the number of strides needed to complete the distance to one thousand four hundred and twenty-nine strides, a not inconsiderable saving of seventy-one strides. Assuming that he maintained the same rate of stride as previously this saving would allow him to run his race much faster than before. A four minute run would become one of three minutes forty-eight seconds, a huge gain!

Don't you find it incredible that such a small change to his form could produce such a massive result? Yet you shouldn't. This physical example merely demonstrates, and graphically, the principle we should all employ with regard to everything we tackle in life. That is that we should seek to improve by just a little every day. It needn't be much but think of each day as that 5 centimetres per stride then consider how many tens of thousands of strides you will make in a lifetime! Each 5 centimetres may not appear to be significant in isolation but when added together the result will be life's equivalent of the difference between a gold medal run and a no medal one.

Are you striding to victory?

POWER POINT - *"Small changes bring huge rewards."*

I find that sports stories and examples like this are terrific motivators. The point being that, because sport is played out in front of vast crowds and worldwide TV audiences, everyone can see and experience what is happening. It's like an entire lifetime of emotion is packed into the one event. Then people can look at the background of the great champions and see how many found success against all odds and in the face of apparently insurmountable obstacles. Such stars become folk heroes. You'll often hear them talk of 'having made sacrifices' to get to the pinnacle of their sport or profession.

But it is the common people who make these stars into sporting legends who are the ones who truly make sacrifices. They are confronted with real life dramas and difficulties on a daily basis; their struggles to just survive happen in private, not in huge arenas and broadcast to millions around the world. These are the real heroes.

Not much irritates me but successful sport's stars or busy entrepreneurs who continually talk of the sacrifices they have made to get to the top sure do. Why? Because they have not made any sacrifices, what they have made are choices.

We all make choices as to how we'll spend our time, what we'll do, where we'll go and when. And the reality is that we choose to do those things which we most enjoy and which we most want to do. For the average person that means choosing to live like most other folks do – grow up, go to college, get a job (hopefully), go to the pub, party, get married, have kids, share dinner together, weekends, holidays, watch TV and enjoy those hobbies and pursuits which they most enjoy ... which they therefore choose to do!

The only difference with a super achiever, be they sports star or otherwise, is that they are determinedly focussed on one goal and they therefore choose not to follow the herd and do as everyone else does but choose instead to spend all their time pursuing their dream.

POWER POINT - *"Choose to pursue your dream and do the thing you most enjoy."*

Oh yea, they may well do some of the 'ordinary' things too but they mainly choose (in the case of athletes) to put in the hurt and grunt of the long hours of physical exercise or (in the case of a determined entrepreneur) the endless hours of work ... because it's what they choose to do! And they choose to do it because it's the one activity which they most enjoy.

Yes, incredible as it may sound to those not of an athletic or entrepreneurial bent or focussed solely on achieving excellence in some other area, the pain inherent in striving to be 'the best' gives great pleasure. Believe me, I've done it! And I still do enjoy a gruelling training slog or a draining business endeavour over anything else. Yes, it's fun. And to repeat my message – I do it because it's what I most enjoy and that's why I've chosen to do it.

Also, it's the doing of the activity, not the completion of it, which gives the greatest pleasure and satisfaction. So, why would I, or any dedicated athlete or entrepreneur, choose to do anything other than, or stop doing, the thing that gives us the greatest pleasure? Of course we wouldn't.

So for these stars of sport or enterprise there is no such thing as sacrifice in this respect. There is no sacrifice in not going to the parties, not being with their families or whatever because if being in those places, doing those things was what mattered most to them then that's what they would be doing. But no, they choose to pursue their sport or endeavour because they relish the daily challenge and inherent pain.

So what is sacrifice then, real sacrifice? I'll tell you. Sacrifice occurs when a person has no choice but to do something extremely unpleasant. Usually something which will cause them personal hurt, pain, distress or even death but which will benefit some other human being(s). You'll find sacrifice at the cemetary. Row on row of war graves of men and women who did not want to suffer, did not choose to die, but died, not for recognition nor reward, but out of a sense of duty and because it was the right thing to do.

The right thing for you to do is to choose to be the best that you can be in all that you do. If you are set on being a sports star then by all means pursue that dream But whatever your goal, athletic or otherwise, first and foremost aim to be your best self every day and to make every day your best day.

POWER POINT - *"Make every day your best day."*

Chapter 7

YOUR BEST DAY IN LIFE

Amongst the many possible answers people may give to the, "When was your best day in life?" question, all of the following would probably rank highly -

* Births, engagements, marriages.

* First day at school, college, graduation.

* Winning prizes, awards, competitions.

* First day at work, pay rise, promotion, new job, retirement.

* Outstanding vacations, good times with family and friends.

- and a host of others too numerous to list here.

Yet, in spite of the fact that I have experienced and enjoyed most of the above and more, none of them would be my answer to, "When was your best day?"

No, my answer would be - "Today!"

Why? Because all and any of such events as those mentioned are in the past. Memorable they may be but memories are all they are. They were real, I know that, I was there. But now, only the memory is in the here and now. Just like plans or ideas I may have regarding future events, they exist only in my mind. I've enjoyed many best days and, hopefully, will celebrate many more; but for now only today can be my best day.

I awaken each day and say out aloud, "Today is the best day of my life!", then set about making it just that.

POWER POINT - *"Tell yourself every day – 'Today is the best day of my life' – then go about making it so."*

I don't try to better a previous day or create better experiences in it, that's not realistic. Anyway it's pointless. I only try to do my best and better my best self. My 'cheerful, grateful and helpful to others' mode kicks in straight away. It has been in automatic 'on' position for many years now. I believe it exudes my calm self-confidence and enthusiasm for life. So that's the mood which prevails.

When I behave so in all that I think, say and do then I know that, when the time comes to lay my head on the pillow at night, I will have been true to myself. My deep inner spirit will rejoice in the kindness and happiness I have (hopefully) spread in and around me. And, if asked, "When was your best day?" I'll be able to easily respond, "Today!"

.... and your best day will be further enhanced when you look to your physical fitness and put in some work in that direction.

Chapter 8

FLEXING YOUR MUSCLES

I have written elsewhere that there's nothing you do in life which you won't do better by being physically fit.

Take a minute to give yourself a long, hard look in the mirror. Chances are you're not really satisfied with what you see. You don't like to admit it but those midnight snacks and junk food binges have finally caught up with you.

As a solution you can cover up every mirror in the house or you can resolve to become physically fit. The catch is that few things in life come easy and exercise is no exception. In order to create a body like you've never had before you must make the effort. The good news is that, with a sincere desire and dedication, you can do it. Yes you can!

People generally have a particular desire to reduce pot bellies, eliminate love handles and improve posture. Regular exercise and following a complete fitness plan can deal with all of that and give you -

* An improved, healthy posture

* A conditioned body with muscle tone

* Muscular endurance and stamina

* A shapely, active looking figure

* Strength and vigour

* Flexibility

Regular exercise and self discipline will not necessarily give you the body of your dreams but it will help you to physically look your best. It will also improve your mental outlook. When you look good, you feel good!

For millions of people, a normal day of largely sedentary work is an exhausting experience. It requires virtually one hundred percent of their available energy, leaving them only enough to occasionally change the channel on the television or fix themselves a snack. As a result, many people get far less out of life than they might if only they had more energy.

This need for more energy is one of the best answers to the question, "Why be fit?" A person with a good degree of physical fitness will use only sixty to seventy percent of his or her energy capacity for routine daily activities. All the rest, some thirty or forty percent, will be available for recreational and other activities.

But that's only the beginning. People who are physically fit are generally healthier. And when they do get sick, they usually recover faster. Often physically fit people are more attractive. They have less fat and more muscle and their skin may have that healthy glow that comes from regular exercise. Often too, a physically fit person is sharper mentally and able to do his or her work more efficiently.

Physical fitness also brings with it a certain pride and sense of well-being. And when your body and mind are functioning as they were meant to function, you simply feel better all over. What's more, by being physically fit you'll not only get more out life, you'll also greatly improve your chances of living and enjoying life longer.

Unfortunately, since it's possible to exist without being physically fit, many people consider fitness to be a non essential extra, something it would be nice to have if they could spare the time for it but not one of life's true necessities. Or they see it as something that's fine for other people but not for them.

Nothing could be further from the truth. We live in a society where exercise for many is the exception not the rule. And when the human body is not active, it inevitably degenerates. The muscles become weak and flabby, the joints begin to stiffen, and the lungs and heart become steadily less efficient. Or to put it another way, as far as your body is concerned, if you don't use it, you lose it!

Because of this, the choice is not between being fit and not being fit. The choice is between being fit or allowing your body to degenerate. Which do you prefer? Exercise and fitness are too important to be put off for lack of time. Make time!

POWER POINT - *"Make time for physical exercise to sharpen your body – and mind!"*

A vigourous twenty minute work out just three times a week, that's one hour a week in total, is all it takes to establish a basic level of fitness. More is better of course (I do half an hour every day minimum) but you can gradually increase your effort. Concentrate mainly on cardio-vascular exercise (heart, lungs and traction system) by walking, jogging, cycling or swimming. And aim to promote muscular strength and flexibility too with regular floor exercises.

Physical fitness promises a lot. Yet in spite of all the good things it produces, it isn't as hard to achieve as most people think. Unfortunately, the term has been so misused and misunderstood over the years that many people have the wrong idea of what it is and what it means. The misconception of what physical fitness is all about can sometimes prevent a person from ever achieving it.

For example, physical fitness definitely means more than not being sick or merely being well. But it doesn't mean you have to be able to play a football match or run a marathon. It does mean having above average fitness or what might be termed a normal level of fitness for a healthy human body – and you don't need to train like an Olympic champion athlete to attain that.

So physical fitness is simply the ability to do your normal daily work with vigour and alertness, without undue fatigue, and with ample energy left over to enjoy leisure time activities and to meet unforseen emergencies. It's well within the grasp of everyone.

Winning Big In Life And Business

Chapter 9

TRY A LITTLE SNICKLET

Good physical fitness includes healthy eating. A snicklet is my own fun word for a nibble or light snack and, much as I enjoy a slap up meal, be it the white linen table cloth and silver candelabra of the formal dinner or the homely checkered cloth of the beach esplanade trattoria, snickling is my absolute favourite way of eating!

Snickling is to take small bites of tasty morsels regularly throughout the day rather than having set, sit down meals. It's a great way to eat. It permits me to enjoy a vast variety of food, nutrients and flavours as my snicklet can be absolutely anything – breads, biscuits, cheeses, cereals, cold meats, fish, fresh fruits and vegetables, whatever – and all can be popped in my mouth in an easy, unhurried way. Eating thus it still works out that in any day I consume a varied and balanced diet and the equivalent of one substantive meal. It's just that the courses are broken down into several snickling sessions which are spread throughout the day.

With snickling I can eat a little as and when I want. I eat less this way but stay well nourished, I never feel stuffed nor uncomfortable. And it's healthy! Countless journals, reports and studies and the opinion of medics and dietary consultants conclude that keeping your stomach turning over steadily in this way is far preferable to filling it. And the fact that in my case it's all fresh Mediterranean food makes it better still.

This isn't to say that my snickling doesn't include some actual sit down meals with family and friends. I enjoy meal time social interaction and would never be without it but, other than a couple of times a week, I limit my intake at such meals to light foods and small helpings. This makes for pleasant eating experiences. I savour the full flavour of what I eat and enjoy the added bonus that, when I do partake of a larger meal, I derive greater pleasure from it.

Drinking of course is important too. I consume frequent cups of tea and coffee, out of this world orange juice from our own home grown oranges and sip water continuously. Wine is my special treat which waits until unwinding time in the evening. All are part of my snickling routine.

The snickling is also integral to my business day. After all working and eating intermingle. So, over the years, I've developed a snicklet approach to my professional endeavours too whereby I work in small snatches, take frequent brief breaks and concentrate on high calibre production rather than volume churned out through concentrated long bouts of work. The result is outstanding.

Conducting my work in this way allows me to digest incoming information, reports and the like in small parts (easier learning) and getting up regularly from my creative work breaks up my day and allows me to perform in a relaxed and easy way which produces higher quality output and more of it.

POWER POINT - *"Live a relaxed life to produce higher quality results and more of them."*

My snickling regime is in reality a total life style solution which incorporates eat, work, rest and play (yes I slip that in too) of which the fundamental principle is 'little and often in all things and on a regular basis'. It's a fun way to operate.

POWER POINT - *"Snickling all day makes for fun, rest and play!"*

I highly recommend that you try a little snicklet!

Chapter 10

DARK LOCHNAGAR

My favourite Scottish mountain is Lochnagar – yes, it's a mountain, but named after the lochan (small loch) which sits in the basin of its massive, central corrie. The floor of the corrie, shielded by six hundred foot high cliffs on three sides, rarely catches the full light of the sun. It's a dark, foreboding place.

Lochnagar was the first mountain I ascended. I was eight at the time and it's the one I've climbed more often than any other. It's an awesome place, wild and alluring. Lord Byron loved the mountain too. He wrote -

England, thy beauties are tame and domestic

To one who has roamed over mountains afar

I long for the crags that are rugged and sombre

The steep frowning glory of dark Lochnagar

Beautiful words to describe a haunting place, and totally apt.

It was cold, brisk and windless as I set off in the early morning mist from my base at the foot of Lochnagar towards 'the Black Spout', my chosen climb to the summit. I knew to expect far less benign conditions further on but I was well equipped with ice axes, crampons and full Arctic survival gear. I would need them. Conditions on the summit can be subarctic and the Black Spout is particularly dangerous after heavy snow or during thaw conditions. Sure enough, the weather soon closed in. Long before I crested the ridge at the top of the gully, a full blizzard was blowing. I made it to the mountain top and snuggled down behind the boulders to hungrily devour my Kendal Cake energy bars and hot soup. Then it was time to get off the mountain. I had no intention of snow-holing overnight in those conditions.

I soon headed down towards the lower summit and its cairn which was the marker I needed to hit en route to a safe descent. In poor, or nil as was my case, visibility, precise navigation was necessary to reach it as the direct line took me close to the top of the six hundred foot cliffs and ice overhangs on my left. But, after half an hour of struggling through the thigh high snow, there was no sign of the cairn.

I knew that I had missed it, either to the left or to the right. There was only one safe choice. I made a ninety degree turn to my right. This because, if I had missed the marker to the right, then I was not in danger of going over the cliff edge. By turning right I would be walking further from that particular danger. I was familiar with the terrain there and knew I could make it safely off the mountain that way.

But, had I missed the marker to the left, then I was perilously close to the cliffs, perhaps already on an ice overhang and in deadly danger. So I made my right turn and slogged on. In just fifteen minutes the marker appeared. I had indeed missed it to the left. I had without question been absolutely on the cliff edge! I probably escaped tragedy that day by just yards, maybe only inches. My experience, my intuition, my gut instinct saved me.

POWER POINT - *"Trust your gut feelings, they will serve you well."*

Three hours later I emerged below the snow line ... into brilliant, late afternoon sunshine. It was as if the heavens were welcoming me back, assuring me that I'd not only survived but that I'd passed the test set me. It was, of course, a challenge I had willingly taken on. One which had stretched me to the limit and rewarded me handsomely because of that. The sense of self-reliance and achievement I experienced was immense.

POWER POINT - *"To fully experience life, push yourself to your limit - and then a bit more."*

I'd never insist that you do as I did (but boy it's exhilarating)! I do suggest however that you tackle life as an adventure. Push yourself to do more, go further, breathe harder, be better. Nothing was ever achieved through being timid, through avoiding risk. Life, real life, is not for the faint hearted.

So do you hold back or press ahead? Turn to your left or to your right? Only you can know. Your own dark Lochnagar lurks within you and is waiting to be conquered.

Chapter 11

A CORNER OF PARADISE

McDougall's corner of paradise was that part in the glen where the river formed a still, dark pool below the waters cascading from the rocks high up on the mountainside. Here McDougall knew that the salmon lurked and he was adept at tempting them on to his hook with the flies which he tied himself from grouse feathers during the dark days of winter. He earned a modest income selling his flies to visitors and the salmon he hooked to local bars and restaurants. He asked for no more in life and was never happier than when casting his line on the waters in the long gloaming of summer evenings.

McDougall was not only the most enthusiastic of all the local fisherman, he was also the most prolific. While others would stand waist deep in the icy water for hours on end and with little to show for their efforts, he would land the silver beauties almost at will. His ghillie's bag was inevitably packed full as he headed homewards. But he was generous to the others, always giving them a fish to take home to their loved ones for a delicious supper and justification of their hours spent by the river.

So McDougall was more than taken aback when, one day, he was approached by a 'committee' of local men complaining that he had cornered the market in catching salmon. They demanded that he share his catches more fully with all of them. Under threat of being marginalised in the community, and worse, McDougall reluctantly agreed. He reasoned that he would still have enough left over from his regular catches to feed himself and earn an, albeit reduced, income from sales. Soon however, the villagers demanded more, and then more. McDougall found himself supplying the entire village with salmon while having none left for himself. He still enjoyed the actual fishing, it was his passion; but he couldn't live, he had been taxed out of business. So he stopped fishing.

In little time the 'committee' once more arrived at his door. They complained that the village had no fish and everyone was starving, "But," said McDougall, "You do have fish. You have all the salmon in the river. You have all those that I used to catch and more. Now they are all yours."

"But no-one has the knowledge of the river and the skill that you have," they retorted, "You must help us!" "No I mustn't!" was McDougalls response, "What you must do is take the time and learn, just as I did." "But who will teach us? How can we survive in the meantime?" they pleaded. McDougall allowed himself an ever so slightly smug, inward smile. "Hook, line and sinker," he thought.

POWER POINT - *"Do not assume responsibility for the envy and greed of those too lazy to create their own wealth."*

A few weeks later life in the glen had returned to near normal. McDougall was once again contentedly ensconced most evenings by his favourite pool waiting for the salmon to bite. Except now around him was a group of men, locals and visitors, watching his every move and hooked on his every word. They were pupils of his newly founded salmon fly fishing school in which the villagers owned a forty-nine percent stake. The fish that McDougall caught he kept for himself and his restaurant customers as before; the fish the others caught went to the people of the glen. McDougall's sales of his hand tied flies increased so much that he opened a cottage industry which employed local people.

For free spirits like McDougall you see, there are always opportunities and there are solutions. No matter how dire the circumstances they refuse to give in. They rise above difficulties rather than allowing them to be barriers to their progress. In fact, they make the difficulty work for them – think about that.

POWER POINT - *"The pessimist sees difficulty in every opportunity; the optimist sees the opportunity in every difficulty." – Winston Churchill*

McDougall refused to be taxed out of business by those less worthy than himself. Instead he used a combination of anger, fear, determination and necessity to drive him through the tough times and find a more than agreeable solution to his predicament. He created an outcome and an improved situation for both himself and his tormentors, one which pleased everyone and improved all their situations.

And he ensured that life would not only continue as idyllic as before for him but that, from the waters cascading down the mountainside to the dark pools below and the salmon residing within, his corner of paradise would be preserved and enhanced for all to benefit from.

Do you possess such resilience, imagination and skill?

Chapter 12

THE RICHEST MAN ON EARTH

McDougall is one of those wise and contented souls who would know instinctively that his life is rich beyond measure. For him there is no greater wealth imaginable than the life with which he is blessed. I tend to go along with him.

Yet, at the time of writing Jeff Bezos of Amazon.com fame is generally acknowledged as being the richest man on earth in financial terms. Bill Gates (Microsoft), Warren Buffett (Berkshire Hathaway), Carlos Slim (Grupo Carso), Mark Zuckerberg (Facebook.com), Larry Page and Sergey Brin (both Google) are others you may have heard of who come into the reckoning. All are self-made men. That means that, as with McDougall, they possess vision, determination and self-belief. I know that fact by default because I know that these are defining characteristics common to all great achievers.

POWER POINT - *"Great achievers share the common personality traits of vision, determination and self-belief."*

I haven't listed talent, genius or education as being traits these men share. Although they all may possess some or all of those, they are not characteristics essential to becoming great achievers. As evidence, there are few things more common in the world than unsuccessful men with talent, unrewarded genius is almost a proverb and the world is full of educated derelicts. No, persistence and determination alone are omnipotent.

I've seen enough of these phenomena in my own experience to know the truth of the above observation but the quote about talent, genius and education is not mine. It originated from Ray Kroc who turned the McDonald's restaurant business into a worldwide empire. He knew a thing or two about persistence. He was aged fifty and had endured much failure before he found success. I kind of like his story more so than some of the tech whizz kids in the world's richest man category. For them financial wealth often came early and relatively easy. It begs the question – are they really rich? McDougall wouldn't think so.

The richest guy I know doesn't own a mega corporation nor does he sell matches on street corners; he doesn't live in a Beverley Hills mansion, nor in a Rio favela; he doesn't drive a Rolls Royce nor a beat up Renault 4; he doesn't wear Armani suits nor charity shop seconds; he dines neither at the Savoy nor at the local soup kitchen.

What he does do is live in a rustic farm villa overlooking the sea and the mountains, drive a second hand fourtrack, wear t-shirts and shorts and eat the finest fresh fish and seafood imaginable. He enjoys laughter, anonymity, a wonderful climate and much love.

Yes - I am the world's richest man … and, if you are smart enough to know it, so too are you! It only depends on your perception of the world around you.

POWER POINT - *"You are the richest man on earth – you just need to be smart enough to know it."*

Chapter 13

ROLLING INTO A NEW TOWN

You know how you sometimes roll into a new town and instantly fall in love with it, knowing that however long you spend there will never be enough? Well Cumbernauld is not one of them. It appears to have been built from reinforced porridge by deranged drunkards on a spaghetti bender.

The original village is positioned in Scotland's central belt. It was developed as a new town in post World War II years to provide much needed housing to relieve the chronic shortage being experienced in the nearby city of Glasgow.

Separation of people and cars was a major element of the first town master plan. Cumbernauld pioneered designs for underpasses and pedestrian footbridges as well as segregated footpaths. The underpasses however collect litter, smell like public toilets and are where local youths congregate to shoot the breeze – or worse. Pedestrians wisely choose to avoid them. They also prefer to risk life and limb crossing the highways rather than take the tediously lengthy detours over the footbridges.

The entire town centre, a mammoth building which houses 'everything' under one roof, was voted the worst building in the country and won a public nomination for its demolition; the confusing layout of it and the rest of the town being an abiding source of frustration for visitors and residents alike. Yes, Cumbernauld is widely regarded as one of the ugliest and least-loved examples of post-war design in Britain.

Of course it is the passage of time which has exposed these serious defects. At the time of the new town's construction, those people escaping the appalling social and housing conditions of Glasgow's slums found in Cumbernauld a veritable paradise. Many inhabitants fully appreciate the town, the wide open spaces, the fresh air and the opportunity to occupy a decent home. Thereby proving that beauty is indeed in the eyes of the beholder and that the perception of beauty is related to personal circumstance.

POWER POINT - *"What is lovely to one person is lousy to another. Perception of beauty is related to personal circumstance."*

So you should cherish the simple things in life like fresh air and the roof over your head. That's not to say that you should not aspire to live in the best conditions of your choosing and in aesthetically pleasing environments of beauty and charm. Such surroundings enhance you.

Having said that - You know how you sometimes roll into a new town and instantly wish that you hadn't bothered, knowing that however brief your visit it will inevitably be too long? Well Cumbernauld is such a place. However, once there you're unlikely to escape it quickly. The impossible tangle of deserted roads leading nowhere will see to that!

Life itself might at times seem like an impossible tangle of deserted roads leading nowhere but remember, it depends on your perception. If you see things with a positive mindset you will find something quite different. You will see an opportunity to which there is a solution to be found and maybe profited from. You will tend to approach situations optimistically but pragmatically, always with a plan B in place. You will know that an apparently negative first impression sometimes surprises; equally that a positive debut may deceive.

Most of all, experience will teach you that, when you experience negative vibes, it is best just to ditch the situation. You will inevitably on occasion 'throw the baby out with the bath water' but so seldom as to be of no consequence. Your intuition and gut feeling will eventually be a well honed instinct which you'll learn to trust implicitly. It will serve you well.

Chapter 14

WAKE UP

When you awaken in the morning you are, quite naturally, immediately absorbed in your own needs. How you feel, how you look, getting cleaned up, dressed, fed and ready for the day. Any thoughts for other people are likely to be limited to your immediate family and those with whom you live. Most of you will have in your mind what you want to get from the day. Although understandable, there's a better way.

How about starting your day focussed on what you want to give as opposed to what you want to get. After all, good givers become good getters. Those who are generous and seek to serve usually attract the most in the end. So the best way to get from the day is to give to it and the people in it. But what to give?

Start by offering your talents and skills for free. What, am I mad? No, not nearly. Going to work just for the sake of getting paid is a pedestrian activity. You are better than that. You should do what you love and what you are most comfortable doing. And you should do it both to satisfy yourself and to provide a service, a gift if you like, for someone else. When you work in this way then the rewards will find you. Why?

Because you really have no control over the results of your actions but you do have control over your actions. So be sure to perform your actions and your duty well. Most people well remember receiving their very first pay cheque. It was a real red letter day providing a (literally) rewarding experience and a sense of achievement. But do you remember the first time that you did something really kind for another person, how the recipient reacted and how that made you feel? You should. Because emotions like that stick with you forever.

You will remember that people appreciated and reacted positively to your open, honest and relaxed demeanour; that inward calm comes from being at ease with yourself, knowing that you are concentrating on generosity and kindness towards others.

So wake up to things that you love. Do things that you have faith in and will make other people happy. Then, when it is ready, life will return to you in equal measure or more all that you gave out.

POWER POINT - *"What you put into life is what you'll get out."*

If you confront the world and the people and situations in it with hostility, anger, resentment and cynicism then you will receive back in full measure the same unpleasantness. Your life will be miserable.

Spreading joy, generosity, compassion and goodwill on the other hand will bring to you wealth untold and more besides. Each day you will wake up full of vigour, your conscience clear, your hopes high. You'll float through the day as light as a feather. You'll dance with the wind.

Chapter 15

DANCE WITH THE WIND

Dance With The Wind was the aptly-named daughter of a great native American chief and renowned for her grace and beauty. All those who saw her fell under the spell of her lovely form and lithe movement.

But her allure transcended just her physical appearance and extended to her personality which was one of light and warmth, tranquility and wisdom. Dance With The Wind was so much more than just the physical embodiment of her name, she also encapsulated it in her every thought, word, communication and social action. She bestowed her light and carefree charm on the spirit of all who encountered her. She was a delightful and rare gem.

Her fame had spread across all the native American tribes, so much so that no tribe was at war with, or a sworn enemy of, Dance With The Wind's people. On the contrary, all sent regular emissaries to be schooled by her regarding her philosophies of life and peaceful co-existence.

Playing on her own name she always welcomed these protégés to her tepee with the same, "Today is your day to dance with the wind and dance lightly with life, sing wild songs of adventure, soar your spirit and unfurl your joy," to put her audience in the right frame of mind for the inspirational teachings to follow. Her mission being simply to encourage peace among the tribes. This she achieved with ease. She totally enchanted all those who came into her presence and heard her softly spoken words.

She would urge her listeners to concentrate only on the positives of the natural world which abounded all around them and to live life in the present. She taught that your life is the creation of your mind so that what you are today comes from your thoughts of yesterday and your present thoughts build your life of tomorrow.

POWER POINT - *"Your thoughts of today build your life of tomorrow."*

Dance With The Wind believed that her pupils should awaken to the cool breeze of a fresh day on their faces and with the purpose of experiencing something new, learning something new, meeting a new friend and bringing joy into at least one other person's life. Critically she emphasised that emotions, all emotions, were not to be neglected. She wanted her pupils to confront a new fear each day and feel anger as well as focussing on joy; none of which were matters of intensity but of balance and order and rythm and harmony.

Her teaching was to find your balance and stand with it, find your song and sing it out and to find the questions that only you know how to ask and the answers that you are content not to know.

Don't you think that the thoughts of Dance With The Wind were not only profound but apply equally today to the world in which we live and to the people who inhabit it? Her words are timeless and worthy of consideration over and over again.

I implore you to heed her wisdom and construct all your days on a foundation of pleasant thoughts and not fret at imperfections. Life is not about perfection or a quest for perfection, it's about enjoying what you have for as long as you have it. Lighten up, embrace life, laugh and love and don't get worked up about things. Life's not always perfect but it's always what you make it. So make it memorable and don't let others steal your happiness.

POWER POINT - *"Life is not about perfection, enjoy what you have for as long as you have it."*

Enjoy the little things because one day you may look back and realise they were the big things. Remind yourself as often as necessary that you have the power to create any dream and turn it into reality through the simple power of thought and action. You can fly when you decide that you can, you can walk on the moon once you make your mind up to do so. Never consider yourself defeated, the vision in your heart is your action plan of tomorrow and your achievement the day after. Simple!

Another really important point, particularly in today's material and selfish society, is not to let things you can't have, or don't have or shouldn't have, spoil your enjoyment of the things you can and do have. Don't be deceived by material wealth and the illusion that money can buy you happiness. Learn to be happy without the things only money can buy and which you can't have.

POWER POINT - *"Don't let what you can't have spoil your enjoyment of what you do have."*

Never think that yesterday was better than today. If you really believe that then pretend that today is yesterday and go have one hell of a party! Life can be like a novel, every day is a new page. If one page is sad, the next one will be happy. So turn the page and enjoy yourself!

Dance With The Wind inherently knew all of these things. She would pass on all of this wisdom in her own words and with her audience enraptured by her magnetic presence. Then she'd conclude her coaching sessions by saying,

"Life is like a rainbow, you need both the rain and the sun to make its colours appear. And time is like a river. You cannot touch the same water twice because the flow that has passed will never pass again. Enjoy every moment of your life today because yesterday has gone and tomorrow may never come.

Remember that a bird does not sing because it has an answer, it sings because it has a song. When you dance to its music the purpose is not to reach a certain point but to enjoy each step along the way. So cherish each step of your journey back to your tribes and loved ones. Peace go with you."

Then Dance With The Wind would glide gracefully from the tepee leaving behind an assembly of braves transfixed in an aura of incredible calm.

Are you ready to dance with the wind?

Chapter 16

EVERYTHING COMES TO HE WHO WAITS

I noted the marque and model of the racing bicycle on which I had set my heart and which I hoped to purchase at a later date, left the bike shop and returned to my office. On arrival there a secretary asked me if a bicycle found earlier in the day parked at the rear entrance to the office was mine? Puzzled, I went to take a look. Sure enough a nearly new, top range racing bike was propped there against the wall.

Inquiries throughout the office and neighbouring properties shed no light on who the owner might be so it was left where it was to be reclaimed; but after two weeks it still stood there. The concensus of opinion was that the expensive piece of kit had been 'borrowed' from another side of town by someone returning home the worse for wear after a late night out and dumped at my gate.

I deposited the bicycle with the local police lost property department who gave me a ticket with which to claim the bike as my own if, after six months, the owner had not showed up. I put the ticket on my desk, postponed my planned purchase of a new bicycle and waited. When six months had passed I returned to the lost property office and was surprised and delighted to find that no-one had come for the bicycle and it was now mine! So, at no cost, I now had my (nearly) new racing bicycle and a far more expensive model than the one I had been intending to purchase. It stayed with me much admired for over twenty years and the source of many free drinks on the back of the story of its origin which I've just recounted.

POWER POINT - *"Everything comes to he who waits."*

The morals of this tale are both profound and simple and particularly so in this era of instant gratification – When you fervently wish for something with all of your inner being, it will come to pass, and everything comes to he who waits.

If In Doubt Defer

There is no question that many situations in life demand instant decisions. Emergencies such as accidents involving physical injury spring to mind, those instances when life itself can depend on a split second reaction. But there are equally many occasions when careful deliberation is called for.

In my racing bicycle experience, patience paid off, but that wasn't a hard call to make. More difficult is when action is expected of you in circumstances where it appears that a positive decision is needed. Yet that may not be the case.

I learned throughout my career, and continue to employ semi-regularly, my 'If in doubt defer' philosophy. It is based on a couple of premises :

Firstly - Simply by waiting, the circumstances surrounding a situation often change. An apparently pressing difficulty today can have become meaningless by tomorrow; purely because today is today and tomorrow is another day. Realising this allows you to deal with certain situations by not dealing with them at all!

Of course you must be able to differentiate between deferring and procrastinating. Procrastinating is when you put off doing something which you know must be done. Deferring means postponing a decision because you are not in possession of all the knowledge needed to make the decision or because you suspect that future circumstances will create a more favourable scenario in which to proceed or even negate the need to act.

POWER POINT - *"If in doubt defer."*

Secondly – Apparently decisive people are often not being decisive at all! They have deferred taking action while thinking through and considering all the possibilities, doing their homework, preparation and while waiting for circumstances to change. Then, when they display their 'instant action', their decision looks like on the spot decisiveness and enhances their reputation as quick-witted risk takers ... but they are often anything but!

The Flower Girl

I christened Lulu 'the flower girl' because she was a flower arranger by profession. So nothing very clever in that! But she also displayed the colour and calm of her arrangements in her happy and laid back persona. My home became an even more relaxed and happy place than normal when she visited. She was that rare contradiction of being both an extremely diligent worker but also a devotee of laissez-faire, that state of leaving things undone that didn't really need doing; or which at least could wait for another day.

Once, when driving her to Bordeaux airport to catch her flight home to London after she had enjoyed a few days of holiday with myself and family, we stopped off for lunch at the famous wine town of St.Emilion. It's an idyllic and always intoxicating location – for it's beauty and charm as well as the obvious local produce! As we completed our meal at the bistro set in the shadow of the main square cathedral, she quite suddenly slammed her wine glass on the table and defiantly pronounced, "I'm not going!"

Lulu followed that up by stating emphatically that she would not go on to the airport to catch her flight nor go back to work the next day. She had decided that the place where we were was just too lovely and the moment was just too precious. She was determined to stay. So we ordered another bottle of wine, lolled in our wicker chairs and Lulu returned to my farmhouse to chill out for a further week.

I totally admired her for grabbing the moment, defying convention and logic and going along with what her heart, if not her head, was telling her. This is an admirable way to live, one which I encompass and which I urge you to follow. Acting on impulse – gut feeling – is an adventurous and often profitable way to go about life. It's certainly exciting, spontaneous and fun. For a long time I cited Lulu's fine example in this respect.

POWER POINT - *"Act on impulse, follow your gut instinct and enjoy a life of excitement, spontaneity and fun."*

Then, many years later, while having dinner with her in London, I remarked on that 'famous' St.Emilion occasion. Her response surprised me. It transpired that, unbeknown to me, she had taken a call from her boss during that lunchtime to inform her that the big event she was returning to oversee the next day had been postponed for a week; there was therefore no need for her to hurry back. What had seemed to me at the time to be an incredible display of swashbuckling bravado on her part had, in fact, been an easy decision for her to make. She confessed to having delighted in making her action of the day appear to be a heat of the moment piece of quick-witted abandonment; she had relished enhancing her reputation as a carefree risk taker ... but she had been anything but!

We laughed a lot about that but also reflected on the importance in life of being able to differentiate between the times which truly demand decisive action and those which do not.

Bear in mind that apparently decisive people are often not being decisive at all! They have deferred taking action while thinking through and considering all the possibilities. Or, like Lulu, they have created the illusion of being spontaneous in order to appear to be decisive!

The Garden Of Your Mind

From a tiny seed in your mind an idea can blossom and flourish to become a spectacular blaze of achievement. That same idea, if left unattended without care or nourishment, will wither and die.

That is why free spirits sieze their ideas and act on them decisively. They know that only *some* of their efforts will reach fruition. But they also know that, without planting and tending, *all* of them will perish.

POWER POINT - *"Only some of your efforts will lead to success but all those ideas you don't act on will certainly lead to failure."*

The tending part is where the exercising of patience is required. But do not confuse that and deliberation with refusing to act and putting off forever making decisions. Procrastination kids only yourself. It leads to stagnation, frustration, anger and to leading an empty existence – to living like a fool ...

Chapter 17

A FOOL'S GUIDE TO HAPPINESS

INSTRUCTIONS

* Wake up feeling angry. Kick the cat. Chastise the children.

* Stuff down a stale roll. Slurp a sloppy coffee.

* Pick a fight with your spouse. Slam door on way out.

* Commute to your paid employment. Launch a solitary tirade at the jampack of cars on the highway. Or kick fellow zombies in the mass melee madness of the tube. Preferably both.

* Arrive at work late. Two finger your boss behind his back. Adjourn to the collective complaining committee at the coffee machine.

* Whinge about – *SPACE* - enter here any subject. It matters not what. The more trivial and the less you know about it the better.

* Stare at computer screen. Abuse client on phone. Feel exhausted. Go for lunch.

* Pig on a cardboard burger and rancid relish at a fast crap joint.

* Return to work. Repeat morning procedure but with renewed resentment.

* Leave 'work'. Go to pub. Indulge in hollow humour with brain fuddled drinkers, junkies and smartphone addicts.

* Stagger home. Stand on cat. Ignore children.

* Rip up the latest late payment mortgage demand.

* Fail to find dinner ... or spouse. Read the "I'm out of here" note pinned to a doll effigy of yourself. Feel no emotion. Show no reaction.

* Fall asleep on couch. Snore a lot and pass wind.

* Wake up feeling angry .....

Read the above repeatedly. Memorise it. Practice it. Soon you will become accomplished in the art. You will do it on autopilot.

When that happens - Congratulations! You **are** a fool's guide to happiness.

Of course, there is an alternative. The alternative is to know real happiness.

Our society and culture have ingrained in people the misconception that happiness equates to material possessions, fatuous relationships and asinine pursuits. Nothing could be further from the truth.

Money is not everything. It can buy a bed but not sleep. It can buy a clock but not time. It can buy a book but not knowledge. It can buy position but not respect. It can buy medicine but not health. It can buy blood but not life. It can buy sex but not love ... and so on.

It is in how we live life as a caring and sharing person that true happiness resides. That entails having social intercourse with others, exchanging love, gratitude, ideas and emotions. Once you understand and employ relationship building as the cornerstone of all that you do in life (and business) then there's really no going back to any other way of conducting yourself.

And relationship building starts with giving. 'Give and ye shall receive' applies as surely now as it did when first quoted those many hundreds of years ago in a previous age.

Chapter 18

THE SMARTPHONE AGE

Just as past eras in mankind's development have been labelled the 'stone age' or the 'steam age' for example, will future generations look back on present day civilisation as the 'smartphone age'? Will our descendants view us as having been obsessed by electronic communication, it not mattering what we communicated just as long as we communicated something, anything? It's not hard to accept that they might well see us that way … but that would be a shame.

Such a perspective wouldn't take into account the incredible benefits of the tool, for a tool the smartphone is, it's just that it's a tool much misused and overused. If today a new sledgehammer were to be invented and become popular, would that justify everyone owning several and going around smashing up everything in sight? Of course it wouldn't; yet that is the equivalent of how many people use the smartphone. They don't utilise the device only for constructive and appropriate tasks. To them it's use is incessant and meaningless and, in the literal sense, a waste of space.

POWER POINT - *"Use your smartphone selectively and only for constructive and appropriate tasks."*

But to those tempted to write it off totally as such, a word of warning. History teaches us that the march of time, progress and innovation cannot be halted and, in spite of the useless chatter and frivilous nature of much smartphone traffic, it is an incredibly effective, efficient and valuable piece of kit. It takes us into realms of technology, communication, knowledge and invention which our forefathers could not begin to comprehend, let alone imagine.

That's not to say that earlier generations have not experienced similar eureka moments when a new invention, technology if you like, heralded changes in people's way of living which would have been unthinkable to their predecessors.

The steam age, already referred to, brought us the industrial revolution and, for an example of rapid intellectual and educational advancement in a previous age, you need look only to the late sixteenth century when a young William Shakespeare with an instinctive regard for words, had just arrived in London. Although printed books had already existed as luxuries for a century, his was the age when they became generally available to everyone with a few bob to spare. So the population at large could for the first time acquire learning and sophistication on demand.

And 'on demand' is the key phrase for aficionados regarding smartphones. The populace today expects instant gratification in all areas of their lives. Gone are the days when people would patiently stand in queues, save money from their earnings for months or years to make a longed for purchase or wait for what seemed like an eternity (of seconds) for dial up internet access.

Be it posting on social media a photo of their cat wearing a tutu, ordering a pizza delivered to their door, making a booking on the next flight to Honolulu or sending for a boxed set of the complete works of William Shakespeare, they want it – and they want it now! And the smartphone delivers!

The question is, as a contrarian, do you need all or any of those supposed benefits in your life? The essential point being that all those millions upon millions of smartphone addicts parading around with the devices constantly being fingered in their hands and/or glued to their ears are not participating in real life, they're missing out on life. They are living in a virtual, cyber world where an entity out there in internet space becomes more relevant to them than a friend, relative or colleague in their actual presence.

POWER POINT - *"Live life in the present moment by being present in your real life with the real people and things around you."*

Ask yourself, why does a smartphone beeping have to take precedence over, and cause disruption to, a live conversation with a real person who is physically there with you? Yet this is the case with so many. Pandering to the smartphone caller in this way, affording them priority if you like, is not only un-necessary, it's also rude, bad manners.

Unfortunately that last phrase will be meaningless to much of the smartphone generation because, by definition, smartphone use and ignorance as to what constitutes good and bad manners appear to go hand in hand.

As regards the 'must have it now' angle regarding smartphone transmitted information then the reality is that there's very little by way of the information being exchanged by smartphone users that is urgent or even needed in the short term. Even 'vital' news or information can be accessed by smartphone, computer or notepad at some later time or place. The bulk of traffic just simply isn't that important and access to it certainly not an immediate requirement.

POWER POINT - *"The bulk of smartphone traffic isn't essential and access to it not an immediate requirement."*

How do I know?

Because I don't possess a smartphone. Yet I run a successful business and conduct a happy life without one!

I use a simple mobile phone about eight years old. It is pre-paid and I put less than ten euros on to it each month. Most days I never use it. I have no intention of accruing the huge monthly usage costs which most smartphone users must incur (how do they afford that)? and neither do I have any inclination to constantly take selfies - surely the most narcissistic and fatuous waste of time and energy known to man.

So you see, I enjoy a perfectly serene and productive existence without a smartphone. So too can you.

Incidentally, I'm presently conducting an experiment aimed at making friends outside of the social media platforms so beloved by smartphone users but by applying the same principles.

Every day I go out and about in the streets of my local town and tell passers-by all about myself, my writing and how I feel. I accost complete strangers with fascinating facts about what I have eaten, why and where I bought it, what I did the night before and what I plan to do the next day. Then I give them pictures of what I ate, the hat I bought at a jumble sale, my daughters pulling silly faces, the cats and Erna gardening and spending time in the pool. I also listen to their conversations, chat them up and tell them how much I love them.

And it's working! I already have four followers - two policemen, a private investigator and a psychiatrist!

Chapter 19

LAUGHTER STARTS AT HOME

Am I alone in believing that the words 'political' and 'correct' do not belong together? That they are a complete contradiction? There is after all little correct about politics and nothing at all correct about politicians.

Comedian and actor Billy Connolly famously said - *"Anyone with ambitions to be a politician should by definition be barred from being one!"* Many a true word spoken in jest. He has a point.

You need political change. But do you want change which encourages ever more state responsibility (politicians just love that) and less personal responsibility. As free spirits and contrarians daring to be different you should be champions of less state interference and more personal responsibility.

This for all aspects of your lives - but particularly education and money management. Both are critical. The former because it is in schools and colleges that the 'brainwashing' to succumb to the system begins and can become set for life. The latter because it is through ever more stringent control of your money, notably by establishing and promoting the cashless society concept, that government intends to dominate you.

Yet they (politicians), after hundreds of years of gradual erosion of your rights and rapid confiscation of your wealth now seek to relieve you of free speech. Not only that but they want to condition and control your very thoughts and restrict what and who you are allowed to make fun of or laugh at and with. This is tantamount to taking over and managing your emotions, of which happiness and joy and your ability to express them in humour of your choosing is central to your being.

As I regard humour to be inherent in my spirit and I base my life around a joyful and exuberant core, it is this denial of its free expression which creates for me my biggest difficulty with the concept and practice of 'political correctness'. As a free thinking contrarian, it should trouble you too.

My perception is that the politically correct generation take themselves so seriously that they can no longer differentiate between fun, with no hidden or ill intentions, and matters which are genuinely not okay. They have been brainwashed so much they no longer have a sense of humour, only a misplaced sense of being offended. Their psychological approach to life is one of everyone making everyone else feel guilty for who they are.

They can't accept that banter, mickey-taking, satire and double entendres are part of our culture; that humour and off the wall comments are an opening gambit to great conversation and debate. They wish to slam the door on these approaches and have us live in a silent world. My conviction is that their sledgehammer approach to ridding the world of the few nasties among us will make the world a very sad place. I can only conclude that they are unaware of the fact that laughter starts at home. By that I mean in two ways.

Firstly – The family home should be a happy, jocular place encapsulating a healthy degree of making fun of each other among the family members. This teaches you to never take yourself too seriously.

Secondly – By not taking yourself too seriously you learn to make fun of yourself and accept ribbing from others too.

POWER POINT - *"Laughter starts at home – both physically within the family and personally within yourself."*

So, as a person of humour, laugh at yourself. Laugh at your imperfections, your physical appearance, your intellectual limitations, your opinions and beliefs. And – this is key - grant others the right to laugh at and with you too!

POWER POINT - *"Laugh at yourself and grant others the right to laugh at and with you too."*

Then, both yourself and others, can understand that - *It's a reciprocal understanding!* One of ... "If I can laugh at you, you can laugh at me and we'll all laugh together." - Simple!

POWER POINT - *"If I can laugh at you, you can laugh at me and we'll all laugh together!"*

Humour is based on the assertion that man can make fun of himself. By accepting yourself as an object of fun then you permit yourself to have fun at the expense of others, and allow them to make fun of you. When you adopt this attitude, encourage it in others and *practice it with respect*, then you liberate yourself from the world of the 'easily offended' and create a haven of tolerance and joy for all.

Remember that in the real world there is humour and political correctness is waging war on it. It won't succeed. Which ever political party proposes to abolish political correctness will get my vote. They should get your vote too.

Chapter 20

CARING FOR YOURSELF

When you look around you at the people in your life – friends, relatives, acquaintances, colleagues – what do you see? Do you see a fan section cheering you on or a jeering section fanning your insecurities? Are they totally in tune with you and your chosen course in life, onside as to your plans and ambitions or are they holding you back with their negativity and lack of empathy?

You'd better know the answer to those questions because you can't afford to have people in your life who, whether blatantly or subtly or unknowingly, undermine you, dampen your spirit and tell you that you are wasting your time pursuing your dreams.

What you do need around you are supportive relationships with people who -

* Believe in you and encourage you in all that you do
* Complement and add value to your life
* Inspire you to do better
* Stand up for you

- as for all the others, kick them out of your life!

I'd reckon that you have all heard the maxim to *'look after yourself because no-one else will'* (oft quoted by my mum) but how many of you actually follow the advice? And how do you separate healthy self care from simple selfishness? To answer these questions you must first take a good look at the people around you. It is the *wrong* people who will not care for you as in the maxim. The right people *will* care for you. They'll nurture and nourish you. But it is you who must install those 'right' people in your life.

Look at yourself and how you conduct your life. If you feel under valued by others then that is actually a reflection of your own perception of yourself. So, to achieve a happy and balanced life, you need to first improve how you feel about yourself. Then bring into your life people who will reflect those good feelings and encourage them.

Most people experience good and bad days, times when you feel more upbeat and positive than others. But remember, your goal as a contrarian who owns your own future is not to be like most people. Your aim is to be exceptional. So it is not acceptable for you to have bad days. Your positive spirit must prevail all day, every day.

POWER POINT - *"Be exceptional, create only feel good days. Bad days are not acceptable."*

To achieve that you first must rid yourself completely of the people in your life who hold you back. All those folk who tell you that you can't be the better being that you want to be. These losers enable your feelings of negativity about yourself, every bit as much as a drug dealer feeds a junkie's addiction.

You needn't live life that way. Your battle to be a better you will be won by throwing out the old and bringing in the new. To those people in your life who constantly complain, spout cynical, defeatist drivel and dump the emotional and psychological equivalent of their garbage on you, pick it up and chuck it back. Kick them and their rubbish out of your life. You'll need to be ruthless, they may be family or long term friends. They may even be a husband, wife or lover. But if they are not prepared to wholeheartedly share your dream and be your cheering section, they have to go. The danger of not ejecting them is that their mentality and the resulting consequences will rub off on you. I have heard it said that distancing yourself from unsupportive close relatives and shutting them out only until you become successful is the way to go. But I don't subscribe to that view. My feeling is if they're out, they're out - permanently.

When someone is not with you through the tough times then you'd be foolish to welcome them back in once all is rosy. It wouldn't work. There'd be no trust or respect. You can neither afford to have negative minded people dragging you down while you're pursuing your dreams nor coming back into the fold once you've realised it. I'll repeat it – Once they're out they're out!

POWER POINT - *"Kick the losers out of your life - and leave them out!"*

Choosing your company selectively so that only upbeat influences are around you at all times will raise you and your spirits so that you are operating in a highly charged, positive frame of mind twenty-four/seven – and that's how it should be. This will allow you to concentrate on joyful thoughts about yourself and the world around you; and to focus your creative energy on the areas of bettering your life and the lives of those who you choose to include in your adventure.

You have to live with yourself for the rest of your life so why not make the experience a great one!

Chapter 21

THE LAWS OF LIFE

I t's unlikely that you've ever encountered the laws of life, certainly not formally laid out somewhere like in a legal document or book. Most are indeed present in the Christian bible but neither that faith nor any other has a monopoly on them. And the laws did not come directly from god and certainly not from some human being claiming to represent him.

In fact Mark Twain got it spot on when he said that, "Religion was invented when the first con man met the first fool," and that has never been more clearly demonstrated than by the muslim madmen who today stalk the earth spouting their evil spite.

No, the laws are born within you. So you know in your deep conscious from birth what they are but often choose not to 'remember' them or are too lazy or corrupt to always observe them. But you should. You'll be the better for it.

The fact is that the ten commandments as attributed to Moses in the bible do pretty much lay out what most of us inherently know to be the basic wrongs of life. We know that we shouldn't kill another man nor should we steal from him. It's also wrong to lust over what you can't have, disrespect your parents and lie.

Mind you, I'd tend to say don't disrespect anyone and I'd also agree with the specific definition of lieing as quoted in the bible which is 'do not bear false testimony', as there are many instances where other forms of lieing can be both a generous act and of benefit to others.

And within that last statement – generous acts of benefit to others – is the most profound law of existence of all with regard as to how you conduct yourself and your life. Because, when you set out each day and make it your priority every hour and minute to be light of spirit, joyous, caring and sharing with your fellow man, you are animating the spirit with which we are all endowed and which feels right in action because it is right. No-one needs to tell us that!

POWER POINT - *"You already know within you what is right and what is wrong."*

Here are some other guidelines :

Live Well

Living well doesn't mean residing in a mansion, owning several luxury brand cars and making tons of cash. Real good living is much more fundamental than that. It involves an appreciation of life's simple – and necessary – pleasures; fresh air, sunshine, shelter and nourishment. Yes, living well refers to the deeper connection of your body, mind and spirit.

You should eat well. The foods you consume not only feed your body but also your mind. So be mindful of what you put into your body. Beauty starts within! Eat fresh fruits, vegetables, fish and meats; drink plenty water - and a little red wine each day. A Mediterranean diet should be healthy and fun!

In addition to eating well, engaging in some sort of physical activity is beneficial to your overall health. Exercise in the open air and take in the sun. It will boost your serotonin, also known as the happy chemical, in your brain.

When you take care of your body through diet, exercise and sensible life choices you will see the change, not only looking in the mirror, but in how you feel within yourself. You'll become stronger both physically and mentally.

Affirmations

Self-affirmations are an excellent way to remind yourself of the laws of life (your conscience) and lead you to do what's right. They can help you to identify your strengths, become confident in them and in how to use them to best effect.

How do you practice self-affirmations?

Simply repeat aloud to yourself your chosen mantras many times a day. A quiet, undisturbed location is best (many people like to stare in the mirror or at an object of beauty such as a flower or at natural scenery), but you can actually shout them out any time, anywhere. In the shower, shaving, driving, out jogging – all will do. The thing is to hammer the message into your deep subconscious until it is accepted as the truth and becomes part of you.

Writing them down over and over works too plus having them on display where you see them at every turn. Forget fridge magnets, get your affirmations plastered there and on the walls too! Here are some simple and very effective mantras which I use -

Every day in every way I'm getting better and better!

The more I have fun, the more I get done!

I am kind and generous every day!

Today is my best day ever!

Note that they are snappy, positive and in the present tense … 'I am' not 'I will be' … that is very important.

The key here is to focus on what you intend to be by saying you are already there. You have to know that you are everything good in life and have total belief in yourself in order to exude it.

Language And Words

Language and words are both powerful and necessary. You wouldn't be reading and learning from this book if they weren't. Yet words themselves are not the accomplishment (other than in the purely academic world). They are but the transition between thoughts and actions.

A sports coach might say, "We don't talk this game, we play it!" So if life is a game, and it sure helps if you see it that way, then you must play it with energy, drive and joyful enthusiasm. Life is not a practice session, it's the real thing, every day your cup final. So give it your best shot all the time. Have fun. *The more you have fun, the more you'll get done!*

But watch your language while you're at it because using the wrong words and expressions can impact on the way that you live your life. It's particularly important to avoid negative, pessimistic and cynical words and expressions. The reason being that what you say can become what you think, and what you think can become what you are. So, if you are a positive and upbeat person, then you will only have positive thoughts and you will express yourself in the same way, both in words and actions.

You'll regularly use words such as -

Absolutely : Brilliant : Certainly : Completely : Definitely

Enjoy : Essential : Exactly : Excellent : Fantastic

Fascinating : Favourite : Friendly : Generous : Great

Ideal : Impressive : Interesting : Marvellous : Outstanding

Quickly : Recommend : Specialist : Splendid : Terrific

- and there's many more. But take just these ones on board and include them in your repertoire of regularly used words and you will *immediately* (there's another one) experience the change in the way that others respond to you. They will become more engaged, more empathetic and inclined to go along with you. They'll feel lighter and happier around you.

And never be afraid of sounding too upbeat! "Fantastic!" "Great!" or "Marvellous!" sounds miles better than a plain "Yes" or "Not too bad," as a reply to "Are you okay?" The positive dynamic of exclamations such as those are themselves infectious. Everyone responds to them.

POWER POINT - *"Always use upbeat, enthusiastic language. It is infectious. Everyone responds to it."*

Interestingly, you should note that opening a sentence in conversation with a positive word which ends in -*ly* (as I have done in this sentence), is more likely to be regarded by listeners as true and responded to positively. This (and many other positive uses of language) is a secret of persuasion employed by sales people and common in the worlds of marketing and customer relations.

So remember, words are a reflection of our thoughts. Positive words come from positive thoughts, negative words from negative thoughts. It is really that simple. Give consideration to the words you use and you will have a good idea of the direction your thoughts are facing, and as a result, your life.

How Are You Today?

"How are you today?" came the question. Without hesitation I fired back my standard reply, "Absolutely fantastic!" accompanied by a wide grin.

As always happens, my answer took the inquirer aback. Uncertainty flitted over her face. There was a palpable pause, that familiar hesitation while her brain absorbed and formulated a reply to my totally unexpected response. I smiled inwardly. I had seen this reaction so often before. I also knew what to expect next.

Sure enough, she smiled. Then her whole demeanour changed. She became alert, relaxed and engaged in the moment. "Who is this person who is actually happy and broadcasts the fact," her inner voices were saying, "Why is he not 'just okay' like all the others? Why do I suddenly feel alive?" Why indeed?

The answer, or rather answers, are simple. Everything in life has to be simple for me. If it's not simple it doesn't work. That's the first answer.

The second is that I'm genuinely happy. And I'm happy because I created happiness in my life. I decided and am determined to be happy 24/7. I make it that way by nourishing my inner being with only positive thoughts and generous actions. I call it feeding my integrity. Then my joy radiates outwards from my deep self and explodes into the world around me.

POWER POINT - *"Feed your integrity with positive thoughts and generous actions. Show your happiness to the world."*

Which brings me to the third answer.

I'm not afraid to show my happiness. I rejoice in sharing it. It gives me great pleasure and sparks upbeat reactions and feelings of well-being in others. It's infectious. Seeing the response which my joy provokes, in turn pleases me and satisfies my inner spirit. And so the cycle continues.

How are you today?

Chapter 22

THE BATTLE WITHIN

While you should not be afraid to show your happiness and rejoice in sharing it, you will also experience those reflective moments when you look inward and question how well you are doing. Are you meeting your expectations of yourself? Can you do better? Life is an adventure which tests your resilience in many ways. It is full of all kinds of unexpected challenges. One significant challenges is to confront and control being your own worst critic.

Not that being self critical is a bad thing. The first place that successful human beings look when assessing their performance is in the mirror. They accept sole responsibility for all their own thoughts and actions and the events and situations arising from them. They know that by being aware of their shortcomings they can grow and improve. So it pays to be self critical.

POWER POINT - *"Successful human beings accept sole responsibility for their own thoughts, actions and the consequences of them."*

However, you don't want to be excessively critical of yourself. That in itself is a form of negative behaviour! So don't be too hard on yourself - but neither back away from striving to satisfy your ongoing desire to grow and improve. Perhaps you have been brought up to be a people pleaser and are trying to be everything for everybody? If this is the case then you need to wise up quick!

Never think in terms of pleasing everyone. It is not possible. Trying to do so is the route to certain failure as a person. Your mission is not to please people with regard to whether they like you or not, your mission is to be self-confident and true to yourself and through that earn the respect of others. Those who doubt your integrity need not be in your life at all. They will by definition be negative influences intent on draining your energy and wishing to draw you into their destructive ways.

POWER POINT - *"Be true to yourself and earn the respect which your integrity merits."*

Those individuals who excel in life, generally impose a level of quality control on themselves far in excess of that practiced by the 'ordinary man', and that's as it should be. Just be sure to be forgiving to yourself too.

Becoming accomplished in balancing healthy self-criticism with a relaxed self image and performance can, like all things in life, be practiced. The destructive negativity of fanatic self assessment can be controlled and eliminated. Managing the feelings is the first step. Realise that you're not perfect (who in the world is)? Just strive to be your best self. Practice and prepare yourself diligently for all that you do. That will allow you to deliver exceptional experiences for others and you'll be known for your integrity and dependability as a relative, friend or colleague.

The only thing that can make you feel worse about being your own worst critic is starting to criticise yourself about how you are your own worst critic! So don't try to fight it, suppress or deny it. Instead acknowledge that this is the case and that the only way to handle it is by managing it in a constructive way. Remind yourself that healthy self criticism drives you to grow and develop. It also causes you to be your best self.

Should you find yourself slipping into excessive self criticism mode, back off and lighten up. Stop trying to please that demanding or unappreciative parent or Reverand MacIlwraith-like zealot with his threats of eternal damnation. Start pleasing yourself.

One other point - Don't let self critique cause you to procrastinate in pursuit of perfection. Get on with what needs doing. Do it to the best of your ability now with the intention, and in the knowledge, that you will improve on your performance again and again as time passes. Berating yourself continuously because nothing seems to be good enough and incessantly thinking of ways you could have been better (as you see the desperate characters enacted in those dreadful TV soaps constantly doing) will hold you back from actually doing what you're meant to do. So never be afraid of not being perfect. You have nothing to fear but the risk of success. Act decisively, act now - and improvise later.

POWER POINT - *"Act decisively, act now - and improvise later."*

It helps too, in fact it is essential that, you live life in the present. After all, everything you are and what you do is in the present moment. Ten minutes, months or years ago are just memories and ten minutes, months or years from now only exist in your imagination. Only the present moment is real. Why obsess about the million things you could have done differently in the past or fret about those you have still to do? That doesn't do anyone any good.

POWER POINT - *"Only the present moment is real — relax and enjoy it."*

Instead, enjoy the moment. Appreciate all the good things in it. Use the knowledge of what you did previously to do it differently today and more brilliantly in the future. Life evolves and so do you. It's a never ending journey of self-growth. Enjoy it!

Chapter 23

AVOIDING THE VALUE VAMPIRES

It has been said that the human psyche needs exposure to at least three positive influences in order to counteract the effects of one negative suggestion. This seems reasonable to me. Let's say that you were told by one individual that you weren't a good enough singer to join a choir, then you'd need not one but several others to lift your spirits with a chorus of, "Oh yes you are! Don't listen to him." That would do the trick and raise your confidence.

By the same token therefore I suggest that, should you find yourself feeling negative and overly critical of yourself, then you must immediately balance your self appraisal by reminding yourself of at least three aspects of your being and behaviour of which you are proud and which others admire. Shout them out loud many times like a mantra until you feel refreshed and invigourated, until the bad feeling is overcome and defeated, until your strength and confidence is asserted.

POWER POINT - *"Implant positive beliefs in your inner psyche with repeated assertions to yourself of your strengths and achievements."*

While your criticism of yourself is necessary, desirable and a mental activity you can control and benefit from, you will find it more difficult to deal with criticism from persons outwith. And you can be sure that there will always be plenty of such worthless opinion around. As well as negative it will often be judgemental. You cannot control it but you can regulate it :

First - Never yourself respond with criticism. Never. Neither be judgemental.

Second - Take time to understand the needs of the other person. Aggression is often an outward expression of an inward need to feel worthwhile and significant. Try responding with a sincere compliment or demonstration of concern. Those who feel recognised in this way are less likely to mistreat others.

Third - Avoid the trap of being sucked into their negative ways. Joining in on their criticism only serves to legitimise in their minds their behaviour. It is necessary to tell people how you feel about the way they are interacting with you and to reject their comments, confront them with their destructive nature and respond with happy and positive alternatives. By openly expressing your thoughts and feelings you are in a better position to manage your own emotions and behaviours. You will decrease the likelihood of feeling alienated and doing or saying something you'll later regret. Take the heat out of the situation and lead by example.

Fourth - Focus on the truths raised by confrontational individuals rather than the confrontation itself. If there is something to be learned from their message, be prepared to take it on board. Although antagonistic people generally lack tact, they might at times be accurately sizing up the people or situations which they are deriding. So listen to them (a little) and don't totally discount what they have to say. There may be some relevant points or information of value within their rhetoric.

Fifth - Be careful how you respond to difficult people. If you react with anger, hurt or intimidation, you will encourage their bad behaviour. Such people are often motivated by the response they trigger in others. When you don't over react, they will likely move on to someone who will.

Sixth – As I've said elsewhere, refrain from sharing personal or important information about yourself or others with anybody, but especially so with difficult people. That's asking for trouble. They can take things out of context, misinterpret or exaggerate information and place a negative spin on ideas or opinions.

Seven - And anyway, limit the amount of time you spend with them. Best of all spend no time on them at all. Instead, surround yourself with only vibrant and positive people, friends and colleagues. That's by far the best solution!

With the meaningless criticisms and worthless judgements of the value vampires excluded from your life, you are free to deal with your own positive evaluation of your efforts. You'll never cease to be your own worst critic – and neither should you seek to be. Just remember that successful human beings and super achievers in life accept responsibility for all their own thoughts and actions. They do not blame others. And as well as daily self critique, they practice daily self love too. Together they add up to real self awareness.

POWER POINT - *"Practice daily self critique and daily self love too. Be self aware."*

Chapter 24

MY WAY

In the classic "My Way" hit song, the subject is totally self aware. He sings with melancholic reflection about his life and how he has lived it. While recalling the many things he has done throughout the years, 'travelling his highways and charting his byways' as he calls it, and pointing out that he has tried many things and suffered many failures, he stresses that the important factor through it all is that he did not bow to the will of others but did things his own way.

The words go on to say that he fully realised that he sometimes overstretched himself, 'bit off more than he could chew' as he puts it, but that he accepted responsibility for his own actions, faced everything that life threw at him and is proud that he stood tall in this way. The singer demands recognition for his straight talking and expressing his true emotions however much that may have disadvantaged him at times.

POWER POINT - *"Have the courage to say what you think and show your true emotions."*

Through it all he enjoyed life to the full. He loved, laughed, cried and is ultimately able to laugh at life and at himself. "What is a man?" he asks, "What has he got if not himself?" He was his own man and lived life his way, on his terms. This single fact was more important to him than any other consideration.

And why not? Surely that's the only way to live. If you can't be yourself, live your own emotions, follow your own dreams, then what's the point?

POWER POINT - *"Be true to yourself, live life, laugh and love."*

Much as I wished for it, I never in childhood became the owner of an electric train set. So, when in adulthood I found myself in a scale model replica store handling the precision-crafted model locomotive I had longed for, it kindled in me a nostalgia for those days long gone. I realised of course that buying the replica would not bring back those times yet, despite that, I would easily have purchased the beautiful toy had the shop assistant understood my yearning and made even a cursory effort to tap into my underlying emotion. But she didn't, she concentrated only on selling me features of the product, and her chance of a sale was gone.

The episode reminded me of the powerful sway that our emotions hold over us in, not only buying situations, but in everything that we enact, and everybody we interact with, in life.

Has anyone for example ever bought security alarms other than through fear of being victim to a break in or possible assault? Was a bed ever purchased where the buyer hadn't envisaged themselves comfortably tucked up in it? Did life insurance ever sell without a graphic scenario of bleak consequences being seeded in the buyer's mind? And what about an investment without the prospect of gain? Or would you pay a sports channel subscription fee if you expected to be bored by watching? - no, your expectation of your purchase is one of excitement and pleasure!

So be it joy, fear, greed, desire, anger, sadness or surprise, or whichever of the many other human emotions, it's necessary when interacting with others, to understand their ambitions, fears, wants and needs. You must be able to target the emotional response of the other party. Appealing to emotions is everything.

POWER POINT - *"Create great relationships by recognising your own emotions and acknowledging other peoples'."*

From the time that you are children, you will have been told things such as, "Don't cry," and "There's nothing to be sad about." As a culture we are largely encouraged to avoid unpleasant emotions so your first impulse is to try to escape from such feelings. This can manifest itself through alcohol, drugs, dieting, binging, sex, general busyness or other compulsive and damaging behaviours. The dangers of these are obvious.

So there are important reasons why you should allow yourself to process and experience your true feelings :

When you shut down one emotion, you shut down them all.

I can vouch for this one hundred percent. The reality is that you cannot numb emotions selectively. When you shut down one, you shut down them all. Using negative behaviours to avoid your feelings may help you experience less sadness and anger but they also stop you from feeling happiness and joy. Part of the amazing thing about being human is that you can experience a range of emotions; sadness and hurt for example are part of what makes it so incredible to feel joy and happiness.

Think of your feelings as waves in the ocean. They come and go, rise and fall, sometimes as a ripple, other times as a resounding crash. But no feeling lasts forever. Anger, sadness and all the others are necessary and helpful parts of the human experience. Each one of them helps you to grow as people.

Struggling with and denying your emotions simply leads to more suffering.

Using negative behaviours to numb your feelings is akin to putting a sticking plaster on a gaping wound. They might make you feel better temporarily but do not fix the underlying cause; and they'll only make you feel worse in the long run.

A preferable approach is to let your emotions out. Don't be afraid of them and don't be afraid of what others might think. They have emotions too you know! So take heed of your emotions, notice them and be curious about them. Why did you feel angry? What was the emotion telling you? Your emotions are messengers which alert you to important aspects of your subconscious self that you need to pay attention to.

POWER POINT - *"Ignoring or suppressing your emotions risks losing your identity and self-respect."*

Let's say that you have a friend who is pursuing their lifelong dream of travelling the world and you are filled with jealously. If you take a moment to get curious about what this emotion might be telling you, you may discover that you too dream of world travel. Or perhaps you are filled with anger and resentment towards a partner. Such feelings are often the result of the other party not respecting your boundaries, or an indication that you are not effectively communicating your needs.

Processing and experiencing your feelings is part of leading a full life.

Anyone in the throes of an eating disorder, sex, work or alcohol addiction will tell you that constantly trying to run from your emotions is exhausting. When you are focussed on numbing your feelings rather than processing them and using healthy coping strategies, you prevent yourself from living a full and meaningful life. As hurt, frustration, pain, sadness, and anger are all natural and healthy parts of your human experience, you are unable to thrive when you try to suppress them. Living a full life means feeling all of your emotions, both the pleasant and the ugly; it means bursting with joy and heartfelt gratitude one moment and wallowing in heartbreak and disappointment another.

An essential element in coping with your emotions is the practice of self-compassion. Ask yourself - Why would you treat yourself with less care and affection than you would afford to a special friend or loved one who was sad or struggling? Why would you not extend to yourself the same kindness that you would to them? The answer is that, if you are well balanced and cognisant of your emotional needs, you will treat yourself with care and attention equal to that which you will dispense to others. Beating yourself up for feeling sad, anxious or scared will only make you feel worse. Saying kind and gentle things to yourself and engaging in compassionate acts of self-care are what you must do in order to feel good.

POWER POINT - *"Why would you treat yourself with less care and affection than you would afford to a special* *friend or loved one?"*

Know that experiencing your emotions and being vulnerable with the people that you trust is a sign of true strength, not a weakness. Ultimately, the way to heal and move through painful experiences is to let yourself feel by being alive and in the moment to all your emotions. You can assist the process by keeping a diary, through artwork or talking to a friend. There are many healthy ways to process your emotions.

Of course there are formal times such as at work or otherwise engaged in the public eye, times which are not entirely your own, when it is not always feasible to process your feelings in the moment. In such instances employ a healthy distraction or coping strategy and defer processing your feelings until you are in a more suitable place to do so. But wait only until you are free of your immediate obligation, then attend to it as the priority which it is. Ultimately you deserve to let yourself experience all of your emotions, and to treat yourself with kindness and care.

Thus the singer in the 'My Way' song is both expressing his own emotion and, at the same time, provoking an emotional response in the listener. It is this twin emotional pull which captures listeners. Most feel that they can easily relate to what he's saying, to the fact that being your own man and being true to your own emotions is the most honest way to live your life. I urge you to follow your heart in that respect too.

In my case I stayed true to myself by returning to the model shop and I did buy the train set. My emotional driver? I had four :

Nostalgia - I don't miss the things of my childhood (electric train sets or not) but I do miss childhood itself

Compassion - For the ineptitude of the sales girl

Retribution - Payback to both my mum (bless her) for denying me my train set and to the scowling Reverand McIlwaraith (he can take care of himself) for being her facilitator

And the fourth?

My fourth motivation was to impose my own will and satisfy my own emotions. I needed to demonstrate that, even decades after the original electric train set fiasco, I was my own man and worthy of having my own life. A life lived on my own terms – my way!

And my way can be your way. The same option is there for the taking when you choose to take control of your own life and dare to be different.

Joseph T.Riach

BOOK 2

YES YOU CAN! - IN BUSINESS

How To Own Your Own Future

Chapter 25

OWN YOUR OWN FUTURE

In order to own your own future you must become your own boss and work for yourself. There is no other way.

Sure there are those who work for corporations, companies and employers who enjoy varying degrees of autonomy but none of these people decide exactly what work they will do, when and where they will do it and how much they will be remunerated for their efforts. And these four factors –

* Choice

* Time

* Location

and

* Reward

– are what determine whether it is you or someone else who owns your future. Look at it this way, let's go back to life generally as opposed to business.

Would you accept a life in which you had no say over what you could or could not do each day? Would you be happy to be instructed as to what your actions should or should not be? Do you understand that time, as in real life time, is your most precious asset? Why would you give it away to a third party or tolerate being told when and how you must use it? Why would you exchange it for a paltry financial return fixed by another party and never remotely close to its real value? (Time is in fact invaluable).

Why would you accept rewards, usually just material and therefore largely worthless, which fall far below your own valuation of your own self worth and your expectation of what you deserve from life?

The answers to all those questions should be the same resounding - "I would not accept that!" So, if you would not accept those criteria in your life generally then why accept them in your place of work? And it is only by rejecting them in your working life that you can ensure that you enjoy the freedom of choice, use of your own time and reward for your efforts that you demand from life generally.

Only as your own boss setting the working conditions that suit you and meet your own requirements as regards choice, self-determination and the rewards of quality life as well as material gain, can you be sure to experience in life generally all the happiness and joy which is your birthright.

Only when fully in control of your choices, your time and your rewards can you truly control your life and all that results in it.

Only then can you own your own future.

Chapter 26

TRYING THIS AND THAT

How often have you heard of a media celebrity such as a movie or sports person being described as an overnight success after bursting into the public eye apparently from nowhere? Only to discover later that they have in fact been around for some time in the shadows, toughing it out, learning their trade? Pretty often I'd guess. So I suspect that you're wise enough to know that success doesn't come easy.

While contemplating this point recently I got to thinking about my own humble beginnings for the first time in quite a while and the many rocky roads and greasy poles I encountered along the way. Oh boy, there were many! I particularly got to counting the jobs in which I was employed before starting my own first business at just age twenty-three. I counted forty-one!

I should add here before listing them that I really had no alternative but to set up in business on my own account. At that time I was so cocky, carefree, cantankerous, loud-mouthed, arrogant, aggressive and strong-willed as to be totally unemployable!

So with that established, here are the jobs. I believe that simply listing them in this manner is a far more effective way of demonstrating the tough route which I subjected myself to, and which many endure, just to get to the starting line in

self-employment, never mind to the top in business. Here
goes -

Bakery worker (twice)

Barman (six times)

Beer warehouse labourer

Bouncer (twice)

Building site labourer (twice)

Company rep

Delivery van driver (three times)

Door to door sales (twice)

Factory labourer (twice)

Fish market labourer (twice)

Granite yard labourer

Milkman

Office clerk

Petrol pump attendant

Professional footballer (five clubs)

Sanitary inspector's assistant

Ship yard labourer

Taxi driver (three times)

Truck driver (four times)

Wow! Was that really me? But look at all the experience I
picked up, the people I met, the contacts I made. Following
on from school this whole period provided me with a
complete alternative, and highly valuable, education. It made
me rugged and robust, and I became street wise!

This last named being a critical characteristic in anyone considering self-employment because the business arena is a tough one, a competitive and cut-throat environment where only the strongest survive and the most resolute prevail.

POWER POINT - *"There is education in school and college and there is education on the street. Seek out and master them both."*

So, although I was largely unaware of it at the time, my 'wild year' experiences had toughened me up in real life skills and had admirably complemented my formal education. I had added knowledge of myself and the world around me to my general awareness; not forgetting the many friends, acquaintances and valuable future contacts I had forged. With a heart full of raw ambition I was ready to do my own thing and take proper ownership of my own future.

Chapter 27

WHO TO TRUST?

Part of the skill of owning your own future and being self-employed is knowing who to listen to and when, and who to ignore. The simple truth is that a heck of a lot of opinion that will come your way is simply not worth hearing. You'll receive 'advice' from anybody and everybody. The whole world and his dog will overnight become experts on your case – people who don't really know you, people who don't know what they're talking about and people who are really giving themselves advice rather than addressing you or your situation.

Very occasionally there may be thoughtful observations or helpful comments emanate from such sources but so many of them are so wrong so much of the time as to be worthless, even damaging. I suggest that you ignore them all. Most of such advice I received in my formative years and early times in businesss amounted to - "Give up!" So I formed the habit of ignoring all that and going my own way. Things worked out just fine.

So who do you ask or seek guidance from regarding your proposed new way forward? Are there specialists in the field of owning your own future to whom you can turn? Not many. And there are a number of reasons for that.

The first and simplest reason is that only you can be you! No-one else can say, "If I were you I'd …" - because they are not you! And when someone is not the person actually involved in the decision they are not subject to the same personality, preferences, thought processes, pressures, emotions and past experiences as the perpetrator. Also, because they are not you and are looking in from the outside, their advice is almost certain to be prejudiced towards caution. Which brings me to the second reason regarding advice.

People – friends, relatives, colleagues – don't want to be responsible for your failure. So they are not going to give you cavalier encouragement. More so, there will be many who want you to fail. Sad but true, but those who are unwilling to make any effort to improve themselves or their situation take pleasure in denouncing the enterprise of others and in seeing them fail. So it's best to stay away from such people.

POWER POINT - *"Ignore others' worthless comments and go your own way."*

Also steer clear of accountants or lawyers. These are the professionals who the majority of people will seek advice from regarding a new enterprise. They are, in reality, not well placed to help as regards the entrepreneurial aspect of your decision. In other words, as with family who might not want to give guidance which they feel might lead to failure, so too is the case with these professionals. They can only, and will only, ever advise caution for fear of their professional reputation. Their opinions as to entrepreneurialship are worthless. They are a long way from being experts in that respect.

And anyway, and lastly, never trust so-called experts. Don't even trust the word 'expert'. Especially when it is used by someone about themselves! I loathe the word and refuse to use it – ever.

POWER POINT - *"Never trust an 'expert'!"*

I do acknowledge the term specialist. So, if you are looking for guidance in any area of life or business, seek out a specialist in the particular area or discipline in which you want help. A consultant well versed and better, well practiced, in their area of speciality But a word of warning here too.

There exists what I call 'blue chip consultants'; those who have progressed from school to university, studied for a degree and then gone into practice as a 'consultant'. Everything they know they have learned from a book. Nothing wrong with that as far as it goes except that they will never actually have done the thing that they are advising you about! Plus, they'll only ever advise, never get involved.

Then there are those like me, what I call a 'hands on consultant'. There is nothing that I will give guidance about that I have not actually done myself, bumps, bruises and all; so I know what I'm talking about from real practical experience. Everything that I write about in this book for example, and all my other writings, are true accounts of real events and my experiences pertaining to them.

Above all, I am an entrepreneur. I am inclined to give adventurous advice and encouragement. There is little wrong with that. After all, it is only by being adventurous that you can possibly gain. Misplaced caution means by definition standing still, going nowhere and achieving nothing. So guidance in that direction is totally worthless.

POWER POINT - *"Only by being adventurous can you possibly gain."*

However (yes there's a however) not everyone is equipped to go forward in this way. Some people, however well-intentioned just do not possess the qualities, or lack the dedication, required to succeed in working on their own account. You must be sure that you are suited to meet the challenges ahead.

If you were an employer with a job vacancy you would interview candidates for the position and as an applicant for a vacancy you'd expect to be interviewed. You would actually be rather unimpressed by a boss who gave you the job just because you turned up. In that case you wouldn't have been evaluated for the work and could feel neither valued nor sure of your ability to successfully fill the position.

So, before embarking on your self-employed adventure and setting sail towards owning your own future, you can dare to be different by, just like any other employment situation, setting up an interview for the post. Only on this occasion it will be an interview – with yourself!

Chapter 28

AN INTERVIEW WITH YOU!

Have you ever thought to interview yourself in order to find out how you really measure up to the task of working for yourself that you have set yourself? To find out if you really are the man for the job? It's not such a crazy idea.

Should you fail the interview then you can save yourself the time, cost and trouble of setting up in business or at least learn that you must first go to school on yourself in order to better prepare for self-employment. If you pass the interview then you can march forward confident that you have a basic grasp of what's required.

Here's how to go about preparing and assessing yourself for suitability to be employed - by yourself for yourself!

You should understand that successful entrepreneurs possess certain common characteristics. Looking at what these traits are and adopting them will help to prepare you for both the interview and the challenges beyond. So what is it that your new boss is looking for in you?

First know that – **Entrepreneurs Are Leaders**.

You may only be leading yourself (especially in the early days) but you still must understand and be able to employ leadership skills. You, the employee, needs to have sound leadership from you, the boss!

You must also possess - **Passion and Self-Belief**.

Passion is about both loving what you do and feeling so strongly about it that there is nothing else you would choose to do or be happier doing. You will believe absolutely that you deserve to, and will, do the thing in life which you most enjoy and that you possess the strength and resolve to accomplish all that you set out to do. Nothing and no-one will stop you from taking the necessary steps to achieve your goal.

The next requirement is that you are a – **Bold Risk Taker**.

Most entrepreneurs are natural risk takers and bold with it. It takes more than a great idea to start up in business. You must have the resolve to stand by your idea and keep pushing forward. Especially in those times (and there'll be plenty of them) when it seems as if you are wasting your time. You also need the courage to know when things cannot improve and it's time to change course.

You also have to be bold in getting in front of your audience and telling them who you are and what you are doing. The majority of people cannot do that. If 'shouting about your business' embarrasses you in some way then self-employment is not for you.

And you have to be bold in asking for what you want. To most people it's totally terrifying to ask someone, often a complete stranger, for something that you really want. Your fear is misplaced. When you ask directly and spell out exactly what you want, you will be amazed by how positively people respond.

POWER PONT - *"Ask directly and spell out exactly what it is that you want from people and situations."*

So take the risk and ask for what you want. The worst case scenario is that they say, "No," - hardly life threatening. In that case rephrase your question or ask, "Why?" or simply move on to the next situation.

Risk taking is a part of business. To the outsider, a risk taker often appears to be 'skating on thin ice' and yes, certain situations can be financially and emotionally uncomfortable. But it's the capacity to make bold choices and take necessary actions which singles you out as a true entrepeneur. Besides which, as I write elsewhere, there are ways of mitigating risk so that what appears risky to others is actually anything but.

You'll also need to be – **Flexible And Resilient**.

When I first met him, one of my millionaire mentors in my early days in business, seemed to me to be constantly changing his mind. So much so that I wondered how he could possibly have become so successful with such an approach and I challenged him about it. His response was that he'd become successful precisely because he did alter his thinking constantly. He was, you see, constantly analysing and reviewing things. This in order to ensure that he'd missed nothing and arrived at the optimum conclusion. In due course I followed his example (boy I'm glad I did) and I suggest that you do too.

Of course you must be focussed and unshakeable on your big goals but, in tandem with that, you should be flexible with things day to day. When overly rigid in your approach you can miss important details, aspects and nuances of significance; also opportunities, both major and minor, some of which could help you achieve your bigger goal more easily, at less cost or more speedily.

As regards speed, yes of course you must be able to think on your feet, make quick decisions. There isn't always time to dally. Opportunities can be lost by hanging about. To be a great entrepreneur you'll often have to move fast.

And you need to be resilient too. Being your own boss can be really hard. You're on your own and, more often than not, out on a limb. Don't expect others to be with you or supportive, they'll mostly think that you're wasting your time. So resilience is what keeps you going, both when you get hit with a big failure (yes that will happen) or just the everyday knocks and bruises. It's essential that you're a bouncy person – when you get knocked over you just bounce back up!

The last quality you'll need to look for in yourself is – **A Self-Effacing Sense Of Humour.**

Yes, you'd better be able to laugh at yourself! Get in first with the funny side of things because, if you don't, others sure will. But that's no bad thing. You need to see your endeavours as from a birds' eye view, that means being dispassionate.

From that vantage point you'll see what you are doing right, what you are doing not so well and the things that are just plain hideous! You will see what is working well and also where you are drifting off course. Relax, re-evaluate, smile, shrug and get back to work

Remember – *The more you have fun, the more you'll get done!*

The Interview

Okay, those are the qualities you are looking for in yourself as your own boss. Now on to the actual interview.

If you've been with a company as a manager you'll already know that identifying the stars of the future is not easy. You will almost certainly have experienced the stress of recruiting an employee who seems to excel on paper but fails to live up to their hype in practice.

So, as the manager of your own business recruiting yourself to work for you, how do you ensure that you are picking the best person for the role, a candidate with the skills, know-how, experience and extra 'something' that makes you stand out? And what key questions are you going to ask yourself?

Well you'll need a planned approach to identify the qualities that will make you exceptional in the role. It's only by getting up close and personal with yourself and engaging yourself face to face, that you can get an honest sense of your abilities. After all, you'll be selling yourself to yourself during interview, so you'll be able to assess just how you approach clients and suppliers first hand.

Make the most of the interview. Don't freestyle or ask the same tired questions. Build a framework of key competencies that you know your next incarnation as a self-employed star needs to possess.

Here are the questions :

Are You A Potential Sales Star?

The reason I start with the above question is simple. You might have the finest goods or service on offer but unless you can sell them then you'll go nowhere – fast! I've already written of how my own self-employment rocketed only after I shifted my emphasis on to the selling side of the business.

Whatever other business disciplines you may excel in, you will only reach your full potential when you master selling. No other part of your enterprise is as critical to success as your ability to market and sell your offer.

Are you a self-starter and able to manage yourself?

Ask yourself how your last few weeks in employment looked and request a detailed description of your activities from start to finish. From this you'll get a sense of your drive, enthusiasm and ability to organise, stay motivated and put in simple hard work. If you are uncertain about what you've been doing, alarm bells may ring. Everyone can have forgetful moments, but as a good entrepreneur/sales person you will have come to interview armed with your diary to refresh your memory about past achievements, contracts won, successful outcomes, people and places and promotional meetings you intend to undertake.

How do you invest in your career?

Ask yourself what your favourite business strategies and business books, gurus and learning resources are. Seek evidence that you are responsible for your own development and learning, whether getting professional development in your current role, reading the latest blogs and periodicals, or attending networking and other industry events to brush up on your skills. Look for evidence of associated interests which reveal a well rounded intellect capable of discussing life and business in general and able to have informed conversations with customers while displaying your in-depth, specialist knowledge.

How are your presentation, negotiation and deal-closing skills?

Find out how you organise presentations, what you enjoy about doing them and how effective you believe you are. This is an ideal task to set yourself within interview to test your skills in action. Similarly, you can set yourself practical exercises with friends to test your skills at negotiation and deal closing

Are you flexible? Are you creative?

Think back to past instances in your employment where things have gone wrong and you were forced to think on your feet. Were you quick thinking? Was your attitude proactive and customer focussed? Be honest with yourself, everyone makes mistakes, the key issue is how you responded to them.

Are you tenacious and able to bounce back from rejection?

Look at what have been your biggest challenges and how you responded to them. Consider your own body language, get in front of a mirror and mimick the ways you think you move, facial expressions and gestures. Also the way that you talk, how you sound, in various situations. Do you express with these your true feelings – anger, hurt, rejection – or can you contain yourself with prepared responses to suit any circumstance. Have you always been prepared, poised and persuasive?

How much knowledge do you have about the techniques of your trade?

Do you know what your top open-ended questions for initial contact are and how familiar with and practiced are you in the key skills of communication, negotiating and closing?

Can you be more than just a sales person?

As a self-employed business proprietor and not just a sales person, do you possess a wider appreciation of your functions and roles within your own organisation and understand that you will have many duties to perform? So, what else will you be doing to contribute to your company's success - 'everything' is not good enough, be specific. Look for signs within yourself of someone engaged in more than just making money.

Are you a leader?

Does that sound like a particularly fatuous question given that there's just yourself in the business? Well it's not, far from it. Being your own boss and having the duty of instilling motivation and discipline on yourself is harder by far than managing other people. Fail on this and your business fails. So be ruthlessly honest in addressing this question. Look within yourself as a candidate able to lead yourself and with the potential to develop, coach and mentor younger and less-experienced employees as your business grows.

Are You Passionate And Engaging?

Do you have development potential? Can you progress within all your functions and grow the business. Are you authentic, honest with yourself and others? There is nothing worse than reeling off pre-prepared answers to yourself, the only person you're kidding is yourself. Do you engage others with your eyes, your words and your body language? Do you create emotion and response in yourself as the interviewer with your answers and interactions as the candidate. If you are authentic and have a real passion for your proposed enterprise then, as an entrepreneur, that carries more weight than formal training and a lack of experience.

This is because it is better for you to have the right potential to put yourself through your own training courses and structure, rather than a you who is not sufficiently motivated and simply goes through the motions for the you that's paying your wages. You need to be something more; a team player who will commit to your organisation and be excited and ready to help build its success.

Can You Laugh At Yourself – Really?

You have more than likely heard the maxim, "Take your work seriously but never yourself." But do you really practice that? You should. Nobody likes a self-important sod and, if they don't like you, they are less likely to trust you. If they don't trust you they won't do business with you. So, lighten up. But be a serious, dedicated professional too.

Having a sense of perspective is absolutely critical. Don't get too wrapped up in what you're doing. Be able to step back and see the humour in situations. Laugh a lot. Clients, employees, suppliers – all will love you for it. *The more you have fun, the more you'll get done!*

Interview Completed

Now, having completed the interview and candidate review process, are you prepared to offer yourself the position of being self-employed by yourself?

If yes … then congratulations! You dare to be different and take ownership of your own future. Time to become your own boss.

Chapter 29

BEING THE BOSS

When you first strike out on your own and become your own boss you will, in all likelihood, already know a bit about bosses from previous work as an employee. And, even though you are starting off with no employees under you, you still need to manage yourself. So what you've learned from your ex-bosses is going to come in handy either way.

From a self-employed perspective it really doesn't matter if your former bosses were good, bad or indifferent in your eyes. You had to live with them and should have learned from them all. You'll have found it more difficult to do a good job under a bad boss of course and yet such a boss should have taught you a lot.

I see the bad boss experience kind of like an athlete training on sand dunes or on the beach, as I do. It's damned hard work but it toughens you up for the real event. When you transfer on to a dedicated running surface you can go like the wind. In life all pursuits should be like that - the hard work in the preparation, the performance itself pure fun.

POWER POINT - *"The hard work in life or business is in the preparation."*

One benefit of being under the control of a bad boss is that it can incentivise you to strike out on your own; the 'I must get out of here' syndrome. Working with a good boss can also encourage you to go it alone, but in a quite different way. He will have created a happy and productive working environment, thus demonstrating what is achievable.

You will never see eye to eye all the time with any boss, good or bad, but, whereas the bad boss will simply beat you down a good boss will most likely welcome your views and input. Your ideas may be at odds with his but disagreeing with a good boss is a quite different story from working under a bad one!

We all need to be able to take direction, even from ourselves(!), so listen, be flexible and take criticism on board. Such is life. As your own boss you are duty bound to work things out for yourself and take responsibility for all your thoughts and actions. Be open to what the boss says – whether that means you, your boss, your client or your partner in life!

With any boss you should start from the position of trusting that the boss knows what he's doing. So, in your self-employed role have total belief in yourself. It may not always be clear to others why you are doing things in a particular way, but that's because they cannot see the bigger picture. Outsiders can only see things from a limited or ignorant point of view. You as an entrepreneur (or any boss in any business) may be looking for something others have not thought of; you may be intent on actions that would never occur to anyone else.

Either way, all bosses want what is best for the bigger picture, as opposed to the limited view from one employee's or one outsider's perspective, because they see their affairs globally as if looking at a map from above. No, they're not always God (only sometimes) but they generally know best how to achieve things. So, as your own boss, shut out external interference and trust your instinct and judgement to know what's right too. Then most often you will be!

POWER POINT - *"Trust your gut instinct. It will serve you well."*

As your own boss you will need to exercise tremendous self-discipline. I consider all discipline and particularly self-discipline to be an essential element in any person's success strategy. Without it you will almost certainly fail. Writing, as I am doing here, is a good example of an activity in which it would be impossible to flourish without strong self-discipline. The only person making me do it is ... myself!

POWER POINT - *"Successful achievers possess and exercise relentless self-discipline."*

As your own boss you are the only one who can ensure that you turn up for work. You will have to learn not to continually put things off 'til tomorrow! Procrastination can be one of your greatest enemies. Without an external boss to enforce time management it's just so easy for you to delay getting down to work and to find excuses for not acting now. But there's always work to be done – if not in one area of your business then in another.

So, just like reporting for a 'proper' job, establish your hours of work and stick to them. Eight in the morning until mid-day, two-thirty to five-thirty in the afternoon works for many. Or work flexi hours, whatever suits you and the kind of work that you are involved in. But find the sort of schedule which works best for you .... and then stick to it.

Whatever agenda you choose for yourself exercise strict discipline. If you don't, you'll achieve nothing. But when you do impose discipline you'll be surprised at how much you can get done and the quality of work that you produce.

And your discipline must be relentless. It's not a one day or one week thing. It's 'forever'. Discipline includes knowing that you're in it for the long haul ...

Chapter 30

THE SEVEN YEAR HITCH

I've often heard the view expressed to business newcomers by various advisers that it will be necessary to stick in and work hard at their enterprise as it will take some time for them to establish themselves. Sound advice indeed to which many of the budding entrepreneurs would respond with the "How long?" question.

Well, how long is a piece of string? There is of course no set answer. For one thing there are just too many variables -

* How much planning and preparation has been done?

* How commited are the individuals in question?

* Do they have previous experience?

* What line of business are they in?

* How well resourced are they?

* How well trained?

- the list is endless.

Nevertheless, people like to hear a precise number, have a specific period of time in their mind. And that after all does equate to good planning. The numbers I have most often heard quoted to newcomers to business by their advisers in response to the question are three years and five years. A reasonable enough assessment I'd say as a general rule and being totally non-specific. But these are not figures which I can relate to in terms of my businesses over the years.

To those coming into business who have asked me the "How long?" question I've always responded with, "At least seven years."

Why seven years? Simply because that's the level of commitment I expect from any business person. In my view if you are not prepared to give seven years of hard graft to your enterprise then I question that you possess the grit and perseverance to succeed. But when you advance into the business arena forearmed with the knowledge of the possible long slog ahead, and yet still prepared to take on the fight, then I believe that you possess the character most likely to see you through.

I'd add too that, in my own experience, seven years was the average time it took me to really break through, particularly in my early enterprises. Therefore I know that it's a realistic figure and I know the determination and sheer cussedness which will be required to overcome the many obstacles which will block the way.

So, coming into business, any business? Be there for the long haul. Sign up for what I call the seven year hitch!

Chapter 31

HEART, LUNGS AND TRACTION SYSTEM

Now that you know that your entrepreneurial endeavour is going to be a marathon rather than a sprint, then it's as well to look to getting yourself into, and keeping yourself in, good physical shape. There's nothing that you do in life that you won't do better by being physically fit and that applies particularly to running your own business.

Much is said and written about keeping yourself well exercised and in good shape but in reality there are only four words you need to know in order to ensure your ongoing physical well-being. They are :

* Heart * Lungs * Traction * System

Keep these, your heart, lungs and traction system, in good working order and you will be fit, guaranteed. You do this with aerobic exercising. This is where you run, dance, jump, walk or move around vigourously and continuously for a period of time. Half an hour and once per day minimum, an hour twice per day is better. You will exercise your lower body predominantly – hips, legs, feet (traction system) - inducing increased heart rate, heavy breathing and healthy blood flow (circulation) to all parts of your body. Job done.

You will **not** need -

* Equipment * Gymnasium * Costly sports club membership * Expensive designer leisure wear

You **will** need -

Will and determination

Any space, large or small, anywhere, outside or in

Comfortable trainers – the older and better fitting the better - or bare feet

If you want more upper body action then simply fill old plastic soft drink bottles with water or sand and carry one in each hand throughout your exercise sessions. Anything from a 20cl to a 1.5ltr bottle works depending on the weight/stress required. Some brands of soft drink come in curved bottles which are easy to grip.

I've used this system throughout my life and, believe me, I'm fit. So it works. No coaching, no expense, no posing!

And guess what? You can employ the same philosophy of

Keeping things simple

Working determinedly

Avoiding un-necessary expense

to all areas and aspects of your life - and of course to your business.

Your purpose after all in having an enterprise should be for it to be lean, mean and healthy. So have your business function as was intended by ensuring it is fit for purpose, profitable and fun. Look after its -

Heart – that's you! Stay healthy in mind and body as described above, enthusiastic and positive, abreast of everything happening in your trade, profession or industry and alert to opportunities and change

Lungs – Bring in the fresh and healthy, new business, contracts, people, technology, systems, money and, of course, profit! And expel the unwanted, un-necessary, wasteful and unprofitable

Traction system – Keep everything in the enterprise well-oiled and running efficiently, always active day-to-day and never resting on your laurels

Remember, look after yourself and your business and your business will look after you!

The More You Have Fun

And you'll stay in better condition, physically as well as mentally, when you ensure that your business does not take you over and provoke stress in you.

I love a good laugh and taking your work seriously doesn't mean you can't have fun. In fact, you'll find that life and everything in it goes that much better when you and those around you are all having a good time. I believe that the more you have fun, the more you'll get done.

There's pleasure to be got from overcoming difficulties, shifting the inevitable stumbling blocks you encounter in your life or enterprise and finding innovative way to circumvent them. I myself just feel so goddam privileged to be there in the ring and fighting that I don't have time to not enjoy myself. That's why you'll find me slaving away at my work (enjoying myself) long after everyone else has gone to the pub, gone home and gone to bed! I don't want to miss a second of the high spirits I experience in every waking moment.

I say 'experience', that's true, but I create the levity. It's not accidental. I provoke it at every turn. Those unfamiliar with me and seeing me at work often don't suspect that I am working at all! I can be perceived as a carefree nonchalant by the casual observor and certainly not as someone diligently engrossed in a demanding endeavour.

Yet, as with all of life, the harder you work at what you do, the more you practice and prepare then, when the time to 'perform' arrives all the hard graft has been done. You are free to express yourself with confidence, relaxed in the knowledge that the more you are enjoying yourself the more you are impressing your abilities on the people and situations around you.

Your behaviour may put you at odds with others in your trade or profession but that's of no consequence. What does matter is that you are content, those working with you are happy and productive and clients see in you a good-humoured professional who produces outstanding results. Everyone is happy.

Try it for yourself. *The more you have fun, the more you'll get done!*

Chapter 32

THE FIRST CHOICE

So you've passed the interview and selected yourself to employ yourself as a self-employed person! But doing what?

The obvious answer to that is that you will choose a business involved in a trade or profession of which you are knowledgeable. Also one where you expect to make good money. But more important than either of those factors, and a consideration which is surprisingly overlooked by a vast number of fledgling entrepreneurs, is that you should choose to do something which you really enjoy. A pursuit for which you have a real passion. When you fail to make that your number one consideration you will be setting yourself on a course which at best will lead to you becoming a slave to your business and at worst will lead to misery and ruin. So choose to do something which you love!

POWER POINT - *"Choose only work which you truly enjoy and which helps other people."*

In tandem with that, choose an activity which will help other people. Surprised? You shouldn't be. You'll derive great pleasure from helping others and this will reflect on the happiness at your work factor achieved by being involved on a daily basis with an activity which you thoroughly enjoy performing. Doing what you love plus helping others in the process is the sure fire way to a happy life (your primary goal) and from there to making profit and being materially wealthy – if that's what you want.

"If that's what I want? Of course I want a profitable business!" I hear your incredulous cries. But take it from me, the surest way to achieve that is by pursuing, not money or material gain, but a happy life appreciative of life's simple pleasures and helping others. So, find a niche that satisfies those aims. What is a niche?

A niche market is the subset of the market on which a specific product or service is focussed. The market niche defines the product features aimed at satisfying specific market needs, as well as the price range, production quality and the demographics that it is intended to impact. It is also a small market segment. Every product and service can be defined by its market niche.

I, for example, in my work as a business consultant, targeted small companies and the self-employed. That niche is where I enjoyed working and where I believed I could help people. So I tailored the services I offered to suit the needs of clients in that sector. The work was (still is) my passion.

To me, niche and passion are two words which fit together like peas in a pod. You can't have one without the other. Spending your time working in a sector, or doing something that you're not absolutely enthusiastic about, is an utter waste of precious life time.

POWER POINT - *"Let your passion determine your niche and then both will define your success."*

One of my first passions and my first experience of bringing the house down, in the theatrical sense, was when, as a four year old, I sang 'I am a little teapot' at a holiday camp talent show. I won first prize. It was both the beginning and the end of my stage career as a public entertainer. A case of coming in with a bang and going out at the top!

The next time I brought the house down, this time almost literally, was many years later when I decided to personally remove a partition wall in my Georgian era townhouse. I proudly showed my work in progress to a structural engineer friend who, far from being impressed, was mortified by what he saw. He immediately closed down my work and the entire building. It was on the point of collapse.

Two years, a multitude of architects, lawyers and builders, tons of steel girders from the foundations to the top (fourth) floor and a bank account hovering between life and death in intensive care, later, I moved back into the property, now fully reinforced and magnificently restored. My sanity is yet to experience such a rebirth. Forget nightmare. This episode in my life equated to a full blooded horror movie with several sequels and a monster that refused to die.

The result of the experience is that today I will not even hammer a nail into a wall. It's not that the nail might bend or that I'll suffer a bloodied thumb, it's the terror that the whole wall will cave in! So I leave that work to people who both specialise in that kind of thing and enjoy doing it.

In my school days I excelled in English literature, languages, geography, history and maths. I whizzed through my exams in these subjects without even opening a book. They were easy to me. I enjoyed them. There were also mandatory classes each week in art, woodwork and metalwork. I gained useful knowledge about these practical disciplines but was never fired up by them. I didn't have the enthusiasm to see myself as a Picasso, Moore or Rodin. Therefore those subjects were never going to be my forte. But I did try them.

POWER POINT - *"Try this and that; find your passion; establish your niche."*

And that's what you as an entrepreneur or self-employed business person must do. Tinker around with a number of business possibilities. Try this and that. Find out what works for you and what doesn't. Experience failure, learn from it. You'll come out the other end of the process with broad general knowledge and ability which will stand you in good stead. You'll thus be prepared to avoid the bent nail and bloodied thumb disasters and specialise in the area which gives you most pleasure and satisfaction. And that's where to establish your business niche.

If you enjoy restoring old buildings (and earning a fortune at my expense) become an architect, engineer, builder or tradesman. If you enjoy bringing the house down (literally) become a demolition contractor. If you enjoy performing on stage then become a singing teapot.

And, if all else fails ... become like me!

But where to begin ..... ?

Chapter 33

WHERE TO BEGIN?

A good starting point in self-employment, and one which many newly self-employed people pursue, is to work as a commission sales person or affiliate marketer. In these cases you will have no goods or services of your own to produce but rather you sell the goods or services of another company, preferably a well established one. In this way you avoid all the hassle of devising a service or of manufacturing goods with the attendant work and cost of their creation, physical storage and movement. You simply sell the goods or service, your host company arranges the delivery and you pick up a commission. But you are self-employed, and arrange your own hours of work and modus operandi.

So which company to represent? Well I presume that you want to be the best at what you do, so better promote the goods or services of a brand which trades in excellence, are quite simply superb at what they do and are the best of the best. Why settle for less?

I recommend that you do the following :

* Work, train and study to be the very best representative that you can possibly be

* Work only with those who you trust implicitly, can look up to and learn from

* Sell only the finest product or service, one in which you have total belief and confidence

* Represent only a company which provides the highest quality product or service

* Represent only a company which provides the highest quality training, support and back up

* Represent only a company which pays the highest commissions and does so timeously and without quibble

* Represent a company and work only with people of integrity

Finding a host company which satisfies just two or three of those criteria may well be difficult. More so to find one which satisfies them all. But don't be discouraged. Such entities do exist and, by definition, will consist of people who, from the top down, are endowed with the highest ethical and professional standards. The result being that they create a centre of excellence to which they can bring the brightest and best talent – hopefully you!

I repeat, if you intend to be the best (and why would you want to be anything less)? then you must work with the best. Time spent finding them will pay you handsomely.

POWER POINT - *"To be the best, work only with the best."*

When you do very well in your commission selling or affiliate marketing career you may well, in due course, earn enough to enable you to emerge from the protective shield of a host company and expand into other areas of business and self enterprise. You will have gained the experience, contacts, knowledge and financial muscle to be able to accomplish this with a confidence born from your success. It's a route to riches followed by many successful entrepreneurs.

I myself did very well indeed from working as a commission salesman although I didn't start out in that way. My first business was transport related, an activity of which I had scant knowledge at the time although I had worked for a few hauliers and delivery companies. But I learned quickly and moved into consultancy work on the back of my experience.

I laboriously built up my reputation as a trustworthy source of business advice for more than seven years before a business colleague persuaded me to integrate into my advisory work some commission selling for the company he represented. It was then that my business really took off!

Such was my success in that sphere that, in my freelance roll as a Senior Offshore Investment and Corporate Planning Consultant with major London merchant bank investment arm, Hill Samuel Financial Services, I qualified regularly as an international conference delegate and soon became their leading UK producer of new mortgage business. As a result of which my business consultancy (me) was employed by several major companies to enlighten their sales teams with regard to my success strategies. Thereby furthering even more my own success and my financial well-being.

All of which allowed me to establish, acquire and operate several more substantial businesses than those I had run previously. So I know that being a commission sales person or affiliate marketer is a good way to build up experience in self-employment as well as the overall profitability of your enterprise.

Still, there are pitfalls to avoid in order to prosper in this area. Avoid the following mistakes and you'll find success easier and quicker to come by :

Stand Out From The Crowd

As a sales agent you will most likely find that there are a host of others out there in the market place selling the same product or service as yourself. You will often find that your fellow agents are your main competitors. So you need to differentiate yourself from all the others in order to stand out from the crowd.

In my case, I did this in five ways :

1. I studied to become, and promoted myself as, a leading authority, the professional the others came to

2. I promoted my business consultancy, not the products off which I earned commissions

3. I sought locations where there was no other presence and went there however remote and difficult to get to

4. I targeted potential buyers within the niche more specifically and more determinedly than the opposition

5. I looked at the traditional sales channels/methods for the products then did the exact opposite (contrarian, thinking outside the box).

POWER POINT - *"Compete by not competing but by thinking outside the box and finding innovative ways to get to clients first and make an exclusive offer."*

I also capitalised on the fact that many of the other agents, both those employed directly by the host companies and freelancers such as myself, lacked both product knowledge and sales ability. In other words, they did not work hard enough to be the best; at being up to date and au fait with everything going on in the industry and all that there was to know about their product and how to promote it most effectively. Don't let this be you!

As well as insuring that you are totally prepared to be the best, learn to not sell rather than to sell. Confused? You needn't be. You'll find all the answers in my *The Simplest Sales Strategy* book. The gist of the message though is that people try too hard to sell. Don't let this be you.

My Experience

At the beginning of my career I set out with the aim of creating material wealth and becoming successful. Although I worked tirelessly I achieved little of either. However, over time, through experience and with the counsel of those older and far wiser than myself, I learned that the sure route to real wealth, both material and spiritual, lay not in working on the commercial aspects of life or business but was to be found in concentrating all of my efforts in helping others.

So that is what I did. I concentrated purely on helping others. It is from that strategy that every kind of wealth imaginable flowed. So I can absolutely assure you that, whatever you want from life, the best way to get it is to focus your energy in helping others.

If you want higher self-esteem then find ways to boost someone else's self-esteem.

If you want to raise your positive spirit then assist someone else to raise theirs.

If you want more happiness in life the smartest way to get it is to help someone else achieve it.

When you give generously of your time and effort in these ways then in due course you will discover as if by magic that the biggest beneficiary of your efforts is .. you! You'll become spiritually rich, relaxed, confident and inwardly calm. One fully in harmony with your inner self. And from there you'll attract every kind of wealth imaginable!

POWER POINT - *"Would you rather do business with someone pushy who you don't know or with someone trustworthy who you do know?"*

So rather than selling, instead work at getting to know your clients and establishing a relationship with them. The psychology is simple. Would you rather do business with someone pushy who you don't really know or with someone of integrity who you do know? Easy, isn't it? It's all about trust. Remember, your ideal business is one which you passionately enjoy doing and which helps other people. So help them, don't sell them.

Iain Bruce

Iain was anything but your normal city solicitor. Not only because of his fisher-folk family origins and traditions and accompanying dialect, both of which he steadfastly adhered to, but even more so because he maintained that his professional role was to help people rather than take advantage of them. To that end he would put the interests of his clients first and in his characteristically homely manner advise them in 'their language' as to their best, and least costly, courses of action; often divulging to them in the process what he saw as the less than proper practices of his colleagues which they should watch out for and avoid.

Not unexpectedly these factors put him at odds with the majority of his profession who saw him as a loose cannon and a threat to their established and lucrative practices. But Iain was popular with the community at large, well respected for his practical and ethical approach and brought in a lot of business to the firm as a result. So the powers that be could not fire him, choosing instead to keep him 'on a leash', confined to a back office and without prospect of promotion.

None of this concerned Iain, for him it was a case of work as normal. But increasingly he grew to loathe his profession and those immoral practitioners in it and turned more and more to his past-time of practicing homeopathy. This work had always fascinated him and he derived great pleasure from it. He could see close up the benefits his homeopathy brought to his patients. So he studied for his doctorate in the subject and in due course was able to abandon his legal career and indulge his true passion.

He bought an old country cottage in a rural village not far from the fishing town of his birth, close to his family and friends and the kinship of the local people. There Iain set up his homeopathy practice, discarded his striped suit and settled for a life of service to his community. Not a hugely profitable concern but a thoroughly satisfying one. One where he could truly help people rather than take advantage of them!

Robbing The Bank

Don't however confuse being friendly with people in business with being a pushover. Weak-willed people do not succeed in business. More than that, it is assertive and persistent people who do succeed.

POWER POINT - *"The assertive and persistent succeed in business, the weak-willed fail."*

As a boy I was pathetically naive at times; far too trusting and overly eager to please. It was two older boys, capitalising on my gullibility, who first introduced me to the "You rob the bank and I'll run" philosophy.

Their dastardly plan was to saunter by the fruit shop and, if all was clear, signal to me to follow up and nick apples from the street display for all three of us. So they wandered up the road, gave their all-clear signal, I followed on and grabbed the apples and ... was immediately collared from behind by the massive fist of an angry shop owner!

My 'friends' scuttled off laughing hilariously at the success of their set up while I was hauled inside and subjected to a terrible grilling with threats of police and parental involvement. But I sobbed the apologies of a terrified eight year old and was eventually released without further action. I won't claim that I never again nicked an apple but I did learn not to assume the risk in a situation while affording someone else the potential benefit.

POWER POINT - *"Do not assume risk or liability on someone else's behalf."*

Several years later I was approached to sign for a football club of which the president was the self-same fruit merchant! When we met and I reminded him of the circumstance of our previous encounter he replied, "Well you're better at scoring goals than at nicking apples!" Then he added, "You're successful on the field because you take risks, I like that. But behind you here there is a whole team, both on and off the field, who will be with you and pulling for you all the time. You won't be left to shoulder responsibility alone." It was a smart pitch, I signed for the club.

POWER POINT - *"Seek situations where the risk is minimal and/or shared and personal gain is substantial."*

And when I entered into business I instinctively put into practice those same philosophies instilled in me. I deliberately sourced only the highest quality clients and colleagues to work with, those I could rely on and respect. I never exposed myself to a "You rob the bank, I'll run!" scenario which did not spread risk and share reward equitably between all.

Some people, when they become self-employed and go into business on their own account, are just too nice for their own good. They want too much to be pleasant to clients, customers, suppliers, staff, to all and sundry in fact. They want to be liked. They make the grave error of believing that if they are liked, then they will be successful. Not so.

While being liked is a significant element in the make up of a successful entrepreneur, that is all it is, an element. A far more important element is being tough and possessing the ability to say, "No!" It is precisely because they cannot say, "No!" that many self-employed business owners fail. These individuals do not stand up for themselves and state clearly what it is that they want. Because of that, such individuals do not earn respect. And it's through respect that business success is achieved.

You're not in business to be popular and, even if you were, you'd never be popular with everyone. You're in business to win! It's competitive, cut throat. You're there to create a successful enterprise. It need not be beautiful to everyone, it need only be attractive to your chosen niche. Those outwith there may see you differently. Beauty truly is in the eyes of the beholder.

POWER POINT - *"You are not in business to be popular. Success comes from being respected."*

Once those to whom your credibility is important realise that you are not prepared to be pushed around or assume their responsibilities and liabilities, then they will respect you. Out of that respect will grow friendship and mutual trust.

You absolutely must let your public know exactly who you are, what you do and how you operate – this is often called branding. There is a great lack of clarity in much of the behaviour in present day society. People are not focussed, there is too much clutter in their lives and no real sense of purpose. When this is translated into the business arena it's a recipe for failure. So you must be specific in your intentions and fully cognisant of exactly what you are trying to do and who you must engage with.

When you present yourself and your business in these open and honest ways, with integrity, then all those with whom it is important that you interact will respond in a similar vein. You will have no need to either rob a bank nor accept the responsibility for robbing one which you didn't!

Work determinedly with these principles in mind. Never forgetting that there is, in fact, no more important quality with regard to success in any area of life or business than that of determination.

POWER POINT - *"Be determined to persevere!"*

So be determined to persevere! Never give up. Life, and all the joys it has to offer, is strictly for triers.

Chapter 34

WHERE TO SET UP?

U nless your business is one which absolutely requires dedicated premises eg car repairs, carpentry work, undertaker, newsagent, restaurant etc. then the first option you'll certainly consider as to where to set up your enterprise is to work from your own home. There are many advantages. The first and most obvious is :

Cost – With no outlay on buying or renting of premises you are quids in to start with. You also save money by not having to commute to work, so no public transport and/or petrol to pay for, along with a saving on your general car running costs. You may not even need to keep a car?! Then there's the cost of clothes (you don't have to keep up appearances) and, of course, food .. no pricey eating out every day.

Then there's :

Time – Is more your own to do as you choose. In the morning you can sleep a little longer, go for a run, take a longer breakfast. You don't need to spend an age in the bathroom preparing for work and, as regards commuting, it's impossible to over estimate the sheer joy of not having to endure crowded trains or buses (and the depressing faces of the other frustrated and stressed out commuters) and the wasted hours of endless traffic jams with their unhealthy fumes. You do however need to manage your time well.

Comfort – Apart from the general comfort of being in the familiar setting of your own home with all your own things around you, you can just be relaxed and informal. No need for 'shirts and ties' or any special clothes, hair does or make up. Feel a cold coming on? Relax and stay cosy.

Flexibility – Work when you want, to your own rhythm. You maybe feel at your most productive in the morning or maybe you're a late at night type. It doesn't matter. You can fit in personal stuff like doctor or hairdresser appointments to suit yourself. Most importantly, you can enjoy more quality time with family and friends.

Life Balance - Apart from the family itself you feel closer to all aspects of your life when working from home (this even though you may well find yourself working more hours than you did when working for an employer). The autonomy of free decision making and release from forced structures and routines reduces stress and creates time for healthy exercise and eating. You really do win all round.

… but … there can be disadvantages. Be aware of the -

Human Angle – Some people miss the interaction of working with others. They find it difficult to work without collaboration and validation. Is this you? On the other hand, be aware of lack of privacy. Around the house there can be unwelcome movement, distractions ... there are people. They may mean well but constant interruptions from family members or visitors with even just a 'harmless' "How are you getting on?" or "Would you like a coffee?" can be disruptive to concentration. Can you work in that environment? Is working from home right for you? You had better know. There are plenty of pros and cons. You must decide which ones are more important to you and which are likely to impact more on your wellbeing and happiness.

If you do decide to work from home you really must possess these characteristics :

* Single Minded Concentration
* Relentless self-discipline
* Constant focus

and be able to

* Organise your workload
* Work unsupervised
* Structure your day
* Manage your time
* Be alone all day

Many people imagine that working from home is a casual affair, one not to be treated seriously. However, if considering your home as the commercial centre of your enterprise then it's a decision not to be taken lightly. In as much as operating your own business allows you the flexibility to choose your work location you should ensure that you operate in the environment which is most conducive to your calm and productivity.

Malcolm's Tale

Malcolm had worked as a senior executive for a leading oil exploration company for over thirty years when he was unceremoniously informed of his 'early retirement'. He was forty-eight years old.

But Malcolm was not a man easily fazed; he didn't lack self-confidence, possessed extensive industry knowledge and had good connections. He quickly decided to set up his own oil exploration consultancy. His substantial terraced house near to the central business hub of the city, where he lived with his wife, teenage son and equally teenage daughter, three cats and Ben the family dog, became the centre for his new enterprise. His wife was thrilled at the prospect of having him at home every day and, with her excited assistance, Malcolm reorganised the ground floor study at the front of the house to be his office. The door of the room opened on to the hallway immediately adjacent to the house's front entrance; ideal for restricting clients from any need to intrude further into the dwelling. The study had a large bay window facing on to the street and Malcolm sited his mahogany desk and leather swivel chair there. The whole set up delighted him and he opened for business.

His first day of operation went smoothly enough. He started work an hour later than he intended, having spent 'extra' time in bed, dallied over breakfast and watched the news on the television. The day was spent gazing at passers by on the street outside, broken occasionally by waves to and from people he knew, two long walks with Ben and a prolonged two hour lunch 'just this once'. At six pm he concluded 'work' for the day exhausted ... and having established with certainty (three recounts) the exact number of paper clips which had accompanied him from his former office at the oil company. There were three hundred and twenty-seven of them.

The subsequent days, then weeks, then months followed a similar pattern. Oh yes, there were variations to his routine. These included – in no particular sequence and oft repeated –

his daughter throwing a noisy daytime party for her friends and his son returning the compliment with a drunken gathering of football hooligans; his wife offering him frequent cups of tea, coffee, 'something a little stronger' and highly annoying 'how is it going'? words of support; Ben demanding, lead in mouth and sad-eyed, to be walked; the cats taking it in apparently well organised turns to climb on every surface and scratch their grit and fur over every document in sight; strangers knocking on the window and 'speaking' to him in sign language; a steady stream of women's club members 'just popping their head in to say hello' as they passed to drink coffee with his wife in the kitchen at the back of the house; and no work getting done.

With each passing day Malcolm became more tired, more irritated and less productive. Soon the consultancy was in crisis. Something needed to be done. So he moved the study to the spare bedroom located immediately above the original office. This did deter the women's guild popping heads in brigade, but did nothing to allay the dog, cats, cups of tea and teenager interruptions. Nor did it deter the strangers passing outside who now threw pebbles to his window to catch his attention.

So he next moved to the back bedroom. That solved the passer by problem ... but now everything was so quiet! He could hear himself think – and he was doing a lot of that! Much more than he was doing work.

Eventually Malcolm decided that being in the house just wasn't working; he needed a 'real' office and he knew just the solution. His house, being a 'period' property, had an old coach house at the far end of the extensive garden. This was a two storey building which, in times gone by, had housed the proprietor's coach and horses with living accommodation on the upper floor for the chauffeur. More recently most of these buildings in neighbouring properties had been utilised as garages, stores, washhouses and workshops. Malcolm's was used as a garage for his car but now he set about renovating it to become a 'proper office'. Work completed he started work there. Things immediately improved.

Now he got up each morning on schedule as he had done previously while in employment. Then, after breakfast, he exited the back of the house by the kitchen door, marched the hundred yards to the coach house, unlocked what was the back door and let himself into his altogether more private and really rather professional office. The 'office' fronted on to what was the main house's back lane and it was from there that clients and staff (Malcolm had hired a PA, both to help him out and also to add to the professional appearance of the business) entered. In the vastly improved ambience he felt more relaxed, more at home while being less at home, so to speak. His quality of work and productivity soon soared.

Still all was not well. His wife could still 'pester' him with endless cups of tea and coffee brought down the garden from the kitchen and his children, pets and other unwanted visitors could get to him the same way too.

Malcolm now decided that his real difficulty was that he missed going to work, as in making a journey to get there, and he needed to have only work space and only work people around him when he got there. He didn't want to commute, get on a bus or train or drive but he did feel that he needed to travel to work. He concluded that if he re-established his old going to work routine, then that would do the trick.

His next solution was to brick up the coach house door from the garden to his office as well as the coach house windows which looked out on to the garden. There was now no way to access the coach house from the main house and garden, nor for anyone to see into the coach house from there. The only access was via the lane.

Malcolm's new routine then became to leave for work each morning by his house's front door to walk the three-quarters of a mile along the main street, then the one hundred yards down the next road to the left and then the three-quarters of a mile back along the lane to the coach house. Once there he entered by the main, and only, door out on to the lane. It was perfect. He enjoyed a half hour leg stretch in the morning, meeting people he knew along the way and calling in at the newsagent to pick up his daily journal. After work he could unwind with the return walk home and there were more than just a couple of welcoming pubs en route for him to stop off at for a drink before dinner.

In his office there was no Ben, no cats, no teenagers, no well-meaning wife, none of her friends and no passers by to distract him. His PA opened the office, said "Good morning" to him when he arrived each day, had all his various documents, calls and meetings arranged, brought him tea or coffee precisely when she knew he wanted it, never asked "How are things going?" and locked up after he left at night.

Quite suddenly all was very well!

Malcolm had found his perfect solution. Should you choose to work from home, you'll have to find yours.

Chapter 35

THE SHINY SHOP SIGN SYNDROME

There was a time when most budding entrepreneurs first acquired premises, a shop or office, put up their shiny new sign with their name on it above the door, sat back in their new and expensive leather recliner and waited for the business to roll in. And waited … and waited …

No customers arrived of course, other than a handful of tyre kickers and inquisitive non-buyers. But what did besiege them and in droves were advertising sales people representing every journal, magazine, billboard, radio and television network company in the land; and each one 'guaranteeing' bigger audiences and more and more assured clients and sales. So the embattled business owner paid out ever bigger advertising fees to all and sundry … and waited for the business to roll in … and waited.

But while most budding entrepreneurs acted in this way, a few didn't. A few, just a few, didn't invest in showy premises, costly advertising or even a fancy leather chair. In fact they spent little to no money at all other than on inexpensive business cards and simple flyers, and chose instead to 'get on their bike' (some literally) and visit every single person or business who, by dint of their trade, profession or known preferences, identified as a likely buyer. They met their prospective clients face to face and – horror of horrors –

spoke to them! But these enterprising few were the ones who prospered.

POWER POINT - *"Successful entrepreneurs 'get on their bike' and speak to prospects and clients face to face."*

In today's internet world much has changed – or has it?

Many budding internet marketers set up a website, create shiny advertising banners with their offer on them, post them all over the internet and .... sit back in their new and expensive leather recliners and wait for the business to roll in. They wait ... and wait ... Still no customers arrive, other than a handful of tyre kickers and inquisitive non-buyers. Sound familiar?

Then, just like their real world and bricks and mortar business colleagues before mentioned, they find themselves besieged, not by buyers, but by web site owners, agents, advertising sales people, affiliate marketers and 'gurus', each claiming to be the sole source of the holy grail which will direct real buyers to them in their tens of millions. So the embattled business owner pays out for the latest hardware, software programme or training course 'guaranteed' to produce customers, puts the plan into action and waits for the business to roll in ... and waits.

Yet, for the thousands, nay millions, who behave and wait in this way, a few, just a few don't. Yes, they post their banner ads and spread their word on the internet but they target their promotions to just those niche markets and the people within them who are most likely to want the product or service on offer. This takes market research and work – yes work! And, when they have stimulated the interest of the right people, they don't sit around in fancy leather chairs, or any chair for that matter, they 'get on their bikes' (some literally), or at least get on the phone to speak personally to every single person or business who, by dint of their initial response, trade, profession or known preferences, have identified themselves as likely buyers. Yes – they speak to their prospects!

And guess what? These enterprising few are the ones who prosper.

POWER POINT - *"Do your market research and target your promotional work to the niche where your buyers are."*

To this day, I speak to clients. Apart from the sheer pleasure of interacting with them directly, they can in this way inform me more accurately of just what it is that they are looking for and I can communicate more clearly how I can assist them to reach their goals. Everyone wins. One client or customer who knows, likes and trusts you through such personal contact is worth a thousand tyre kickers who don't! It is a simple sense approach which reduces time, stress and cost while increasing effectiveness, satisfaction and profit.

What business person in their right mind would not choose to proceed in a way which creates more profit for less and more pleasurable work?

But note that work is involved. That's another key. The internet particularly, and more so than even a lazy budding business person lolling in his recliner waiting for business to magically arrive, gives newcomers to self-employment the false impression that finding success is 'easy'. If only! There's work involved … and lots of it.Those who succeed put in the hours, the hard graft, the learning and the education, and then they apply it rigourously day after day, year after year, non stop.

POWER POINT - *"Never think that success comes work free. Waiting for success is a long wait."*

They become specialists in their field, masters of their craft. They realise that their success or failure directly reflects their skill in relating to, and engaging with, their clients and customers. This attitude is the exact opposite of what those affected by the shiny shop sign syndrome display. If waiting for business to come to you, then you are in for a long wait.

That's not to say that opportunities do not abound. They are everywhere, all around. But they won't fall into the lap of those sitting around doing nothing to attract them. You have to be out there in the business arena working, planning and scheming before the opportunities present themselves. It is only by being involved that you learn to spot opportunities.

There are darned few shortcuts to success in business but developing your ability to identify opportunities and to act on them decisively is one. If you are always putting yourself out there, are always alert to a possible opening, always focussed on your goal, always performing to the best of your ability, then the openings will come.

There is no one sure route to success. No single rule to follow. Success comes to the few who find it mainly from bloody minded determination and opportunity grabbing. You never know where your break will come from so you have to be on high alert for it all the time. It won't arrive like a bolt of lightening. Big breaks are rare. Much more common is a series of small breaks, each one a step on the stairway to success.

Chapter 36

FLIRTING WITH THE STARS

My home town of Aberdeen in Scotland was at one time Europe's largest fishing port. Thousands of people were employed in the fish industry which comprised everything from trawlermen to dock workers to fish houses, fish processing factories and transportation. As a young kid growing up, many of my first after-school and weekend jobs were 'in the fish'.

Quite suddenly the industry died. The fishing boats left … and the oil supply vessels moved in. Yes, oil had been discovered in the North Sea. Aberdeen would enjoy a second bonanza as the oil capital of Europe! The economy thrived and entrepreneurs formerly benefiting from opportunities created in fishing turned their attention to the big bucks to be made in North Sea support and ancillary services. I was one of them.

My enterprises were actually two or three times down the line from direct oil related businesses but I was in little doubt that it was the front line exploration and pumping of oil (and gas) that was the prime creator of the wealth which I, and so many others, enjoyed.

In due course my business activities took me to further flung corners of Britain, Europe and the world. Many of these places had none of the resources, industry, wealth and attendant infrastructure which first fishing and then oil had created in the North East of Scotland. Yet I still found opportunities to create businesses. Lots of them. So many in fact that it led me to a startling conclusion.

What I realised was this – You don't need a Klondike situation in order to prosper as an entrepreneur!

POWER POINT - *"You can prosper as an entrepreneur in any environment anywhere."*

Although such a thriving scenario encourages speculation, business creation and commercial activity, that in itself is not the main driver in people's entrepreneurial motivation. Yes, having a ready market and one hungry for your input sure helps, but the primary driver behind any entrepreneur is the ambition to be their own man, control their own destiny and be the best they possibly can be. With that mindset you'll find opportunities and succeed anywhere!

Proof of the point is simple :

One – If a Klondike situation alone is responsible for opportunity and wealth, then every single person in a place such as Aberdeen would be cashing in with their own businesses. But they're not!

Two – Entrepreneurs invent solutions, create enterprises and make fortunes everywhere. They thrive in the most improbable places. Be it deserts, jungles, mountain tops or frozen wastes, you'll find someone profiting from an opportunity they've identified.

And they'll have spotted the opportunity from first being of a mindset that is primed to recognise a difficulty as an opportunity to create a solution. They'll possess an enquiring and inventive mindset and a positive attitude. That's the essential requisite for success. A bad attitude is like a flat tyre, you won't get anywhere until you change it.

POWER POINT - *"Opportunity is seeing a solution to a difficulty."*

Michael Caine, the film star, tells the story of being seated in his own restaurant in London one evening when he was approached by a slightly tipsy diner on his way to the gents' room. "I thought this place was supposed to be full of famous movie people?" challenged the man. "Well, what am I then?" replied Michael good humouredly. "You're the owner," said the man, "You don't count."

"Okay," said Michael, "Then who is that sitting at the corner table?" The man turned and stared long and hard at the fellow pointed out by Michael. Eventually he said, "I don't know." Michael replied, "That's Tom Cruise," and continued, "Who is that standing at the bar?" Again the man took a long and earnest look at the figure pointed out. Eventually he repeated the same answer, "I don't know." Michael enlightened him with, "That's Clint Eastwood." At that the man just shrugged his shoulders and tottered on to his date with nature in the gents'.

A short time later the diner, on his way back from the men's room, again passed Michael seated at his table. This time he didn't stop but simply called over, "And there's no-one famous in the toilets either!"

Apart from the humour, the moral of this story is two fold. People only see what they want to see and frequently fail to see opportunities plainly presented to them. The diner in the story missed the opportunity to perhaps meet and share a word with the stars.

Michael Caine, on the other hand, is famous for inevitably recognising opportunities and saying 'yes' to everything. As a result he has worked in his chosen profession of movie acting, a notoriously insecure one, nonstop throughout the years. He is also known as being a joy to work with and a stickler for detail. He prepares for all of his roles, large or small, meticulously and diligently.

As an entrepreneur or self-employed business person you should do the same. Be alert and on the watch for opportunities at all times. The best way to do this is to have a reputation for reliability and quality of performance just as Michael Caine does. Know yourself, your business, your industry and the people in and around it inside out. Then the opportunities will come your way.

Also be excellent at what you do. Areas to give absolute priority to are -

* **Sales** - This is what brings in the money. Do your selling yourself. You're the best person for it.

* **Finance** - Keep tight control of your money. Personally manage it. *Never* let anyone else have access to your cash.

* **Personnel** - Delegate and employ by all means but use only people you trust implicitly. Better to employ no-one at all rather than someone you don't trust.

Adherence to these three points is critical to your success. Believe me, I've been there. I've also been to Michael Caine's restaurant. He wasn't there when I visited but Tom Cruise and Clint Eastwood were. They didn't recognise me.

Chapter 37

SAW THE LEGS OFF

The new desk arrived and 'Short' Ken Smith, all four feet ten inches of him, sat down behind it. His head barely showed above the desk. "No problem," he quipped in his characteristically chirpy manner, "Saw the legs off!" "What!" was the incredulous cry from all around as it was pointed out to him that the desk was an expensive piece of real oak. But, as the boss and the one footing the bill, there'd be no going against him and soon the desk was upside down and, with Ken leading the operation, the sawing began.

In no time at all the task was completed, the desk was returned to its upright position and Ken sat down once more behind it. "Perfect," he purred as he could now sit comfortably behind it, see over it and be seen. But Ken's size and pint sized desk now put him at a considerably lower level than anyone sitting opposite him. The hilarious result was that guests found themselves towering over Ken and looking down on him even while they themselves were seated.

This situation was the exact opposite of what many bosses do in their offices with regard to their own seating position and the seating of any guest opposite them. Those bigwigs wishing to appear more important, imposing and grandiose than their visitors mount their desks on elevated platforms and position smaller, low slung guest chairs on the other side at normal floor level. This creates the effect of the boss whose office it is appearing exalted and superior while the guest has to huddle, knees to chest and stare upwards to him like an errant schoolboy before the headmaster.

It was suggested to Short Ken that he do likewise and mount his desk on a pedestal so as to redress the balance and not put himself in an 'inferior' position to his guests. But he'd have none of it. "I'm not playing silly buggers!" he gruffed. So clients, suppliers, guests and staff called to see him and all sat overshadowing his tiny figure as they spoke.

Psychologically, such a set up would be considered as putting the lower person at a disadvantage and certainly, to the casual observer, this might have appeared so in Ken's case. But Ken was made of sterner stuff. He saw the difficulty created by his lowly stature as an opportunity to gain the ascendancy. He applied reverse psychology.

POWER POINT - *"Reverse psychology – do, or be, the opposite of what people expect."*

The moment anyone stepped into his office he would briskly approach them, grab their hand and welcome them with a barked, "I may be small but I'm no pushover. Say what you've got to say, you've got ten minutes!" Then he'd return to his desk, set an alarm clock to ring in ten minutes time and pointedly slam it down on the desk facing the visitor. As the guest started to speak, Ken would lean forward and look him straight ... up the nostrils! He held his gaze there throughout the meeting.

To say that he disconcerted his visitors is to put it mildly. All left knowing that they had locked horns with a serious businessman, a real tough cookie and expressed feeling unnerved rather than superior in having to look down at him. Most of all though, they remembered him!

Short Ken's reverse psychology method presented a great example of how to -

* Stand out from the crowd

and

* Turn a difficult situation into a winning one

With his memorable personality and way of going about things he had established a reputation as a creative thinker renowned for finding and employing simple solutions to situations, as in how he had dealt with his desk. Because of this he achieved something of a legendary status in the industry and his approach became known throughout his enterprise and the business community at large as the 'Saw the Legs Off' strategy.

I am not suggesting that you must time your visitors with an alarm clock nor that you fix your gaze up their nose while addressing them (you can try it if you like), but I do urge you to develop your own personality and aim to make a memorable impression on others – if only through the excellence of your work.

POWER POINT - *"Impress people with the simple excellence of your work."*

Of course an exceptional appearance can make you memorable too …..

Although I write books and hope that their covers are appealing and give a good whiff of what my readers might expect to find inside, I've been around the block sufficient times to know that the reality may in some cases be quite different .....

I had only popped into the headquarters of the major investment company I represented as a freelance agent to drop off a couple of pieces of business I'd won and catch up on 'news', when one of the front office girls beckoned me over. She told me there was a scruffy individual in reception asking to speak to someone about 'money' but none of the regular company employed consultants would see him because he 'stank to high heaven'.

So I went through and immediately recognised the slightly podgy character as a farmer in his typical scruffy garb, probably in town that day for the weekly cattle sales. I brought him a cup of tea and sat down for a chat. I soon learned that he had a stash of eighty thousand pounds hidden under the floorboards at his farmhouse which he now wanted to relocate to somewhere more secure due to the fact that his son had discovered the hiding place and was regularly pilfering from the hoard.

In little time I presented him with a solution to his difficulty to which he agreed and I suggested that we arrange to meet again in order for him to deposit the money with the company. But he quickly assured me that that would not be necessary and proceeded to unload large bundles of used notes from the many pockets of his tatty coat. Now I could see that he was not a chubby fellow at all but actually rather skinny!

I summoned a staff accountant to verify the transaction and for the next hour we carefully counted the cash. Yes there was just over eighty thousand pounds sterling! The paperwork was concluded and my new farmer friend departed with a hefty weight lifted from his mind – and body!

POWER POINT - *"Neither look up to the rich nor down on the poor."*

The event reminded me that we should never look up to the rich nor down on the poor. Nor judge a book by its cover as the snobbish in-house consultants had done - thereby losing out on a healthy commission, a friend for life and countless future introductions of similarly lucrative business.

Chapter 38

A SONG, A DANCE AND A SILLY WALK

There are many formulas for success in business and no one correct one …

The British comedian and actor Max Wall, who started his career as a music hall entertainer in the nineteen thirties, would often attribute his successs to 'a song, a dance and a silly walk' – these being the basic elements which he deemed it necessary to include in his performance in order to captivate his audience.

While I do not advocate adopting that approach in the boardroom, not literally anyway, figuratively speaking it's not a bad mental attitude to employ. After all if you are upbeat, humourous and 'whistling a happy tune' (inside your head at least) what better way could there be to approach your work?

Wall also possessed a natural tragi-comic expression of the kind associated with the classic clown face and he used this to great effect in enacting the pathos inherent in his stage performances; as well as it being a great asset in the many straight acting roles of his later career. In fact, such was his prowess as a serious actor that it was once said of him that he made Laurence Olivier look like an amateur!

As regards business, I've long felt that acting is a skill which can be highly valuable in the commercial world. I learned early on, for instance, that the first solicitor to represent me in my various business and personal affairs was a skilled, stone wall actor. In consultations he adopted a dead pan expression and a steady stare which never wavered throughout the meeting. Therefore he was impossible to read. You couldn't know his thoughts. It was an impressive performance.

Then there are politicians. Are they not to a man, and woman, quintessentially actors? The 'best' of them can portray a different character to suit any occasion, a face for every situation and a pose to befit any circumstance. Their public face is often the epitomy of fine acting as they deny the undeniable, defend the indefensible and turn every question asked of them into an opportunity to deliver their well rehearsed lines. Yes, they are actors.

So, to succeed in business, there's a strong line of argument which suggests that the ability to act is a useful talent to possess. And, if you don't possess it, then perhaps you should seek to learn the skill. It could stand you in good stead in all sorts of face-to-face situations.

But, and this is key, rather than working to develop the ability to effectively pretend that you're someone other than yourself – someone more polished, stronger, more worldly, more sophisticated, whatever - why not devote that same energy to learning to perform better as yourself? For, regardless of what you might gain by playing out a part which is not you, just think of the gain to be had in being a better version of yourself. So that is what you should aspire to.

POWER POINT - *"Perform – but perform as a better version of yourself."*

Identify your own strengths then work at the way you present yourself and them to the world. This is what many entrepreneurs fail to do. They have the ability, the knowledge, the wherewithal to do great things in the market place but fail to deliver it in such a way as to win the business. As Oscar Schindler, the master salesman in the classic film Schindler's List, replies when asked what his role in the business will be, he responds, accompanied by an expansive hand gesture - "Presentation!" And yes, presentation is everything.

POWER POINT - *"Presentation is everything!"*

As was the case with myself in my early years in business, I concentrated on the quality of my service and did indeed deliver excellence. Yet I failed to prosper because I didn't understand the importance of presentation. But once I developed my personality, worked on my presentation skills and promoted myself with verve and charisma, I never looked back.

So think presentation, create a memorable persona for your audience and act out the best version of yourself. Present your very own song, dance and silly walk!

Chapter 39

PIE AND CHIPS

There was a time when pubs sold beer and spirits and little else. Folks went there to enjoy a drink. If you wanted something to snickle on then a bag of potatoe crisps or maybe peanuts was the most you were likely to get.

Then one pub owner, Sandy McKay, had the bright idea to sell food. He settled on one simple wholesome snack, a hot minced beef pie and chips, which would go down well before, during or after a belly full of beer. The punters flocked in!

At a landlords' association meeting a couple of months after launching his hot food strategy, Sandy was quizzed about his new initiative.

"Do you sell a lot of pies and chips?"

"Oh yes."

"But do you make any money from it?"

"No, nothing at all."

"Then why do you do it?"

"Ah – you should see all the beer that I sell!"

Sandy, you see, was more than just a pub landlord or even a businessman. He was an entrepreneur. He was prepared to innovate and take risks. And he (perhaps unwittingly) demonstrated three key elements in entrepreneurial behaviour -

* **Inventiveness** – He looked for and created solutions as to how to increase trade

* **Loss Leader** – He was prepared to sell something at a loss in order to make a profit on his main line

* **Incentive** – He understood that he had to give his customers an added incentive to come to his pub

- and in doing this he prospered.

Soon afterwards, another pub in town started giving away free fish and chip suppers for one hour each Friday evening. The proprietor reported selling more drink in that one evening than in all the other nights of the week put together!

Eventually it became the normal thing for all pubs to sell food. In many cases the catering side of the business overtook the drinks side both in terms of revenue and in being the main activity of the enterprise. So the beer and spirits, and wines now introduced, were the added incentive for people to come and eat there!

There was another interesting development. A couple of landlords realised that there was a market niche of drinkers who did not want to go to a pub which had effectively become a restaurant rather than a traditional watering hole. So they made a point of not providing food. They advertised their pubs as being purely drinking establishments. The drinkers rolled in!

These pub owners were therefore capitalising on providing a service to a niche market of patrons who wished solely to drink and specifically not be in a place serving food or surrounded by people eating. These owners too were displaying -

* Creativity

* Niche Recognition

and

* Branding and Marketing Ability

They were prepared to try different strategies in order to keep pace with, or get ahead of, market trends. Better still, those like Sandy McKay, were actually creating the market trends!

POWER POINT - *"Inventive entrepreneurs create market trends."*

Mr.Carpenter employed a different approach. He was Carpenter by name and a carpenter to trade. His workshop was crammed full of coffins in various stages of preparation, all on order to the undertaker whose funeral parlour was located next door. When the undertaker passed away (yes they pop their clogs too), Mr.Carpenter bought that business.

He also acquired the disused country manor at the end of the same street and opened it as a retirement home. And for good measure he purchased for Mrs.Carpenter two nearby shop units which were converted for use as a creche and childrens pre-school nursery.

And all the while Mr.Carpenter continued with his local authority contract work in the renovation of old town properties into modern apartments for let to newly weds.

Carpenter rarely felt the need to advertise his businesses, any of them. Clientele passed from one enterprise to the next in a continuous flow as the various stages of their lives unfolded. And there were referrals.

So Mr.Carpenter had constructed the perfect business model. A veritable cradle to grave solution. One with multiple income streams and a guaranteed customer base.

Many hugely successful entrepreneurs operate in a similar manner. They build up a series of 'crossover businesses'; enterprises which are inter-related, continuous and feed each other with repeat business and sales. I developed my own business in just such a way. So too did Harry Barclay.

Chapter 40

HARRY BARCLAY

The tractors, trailers, ploughs, bailing machines, spreaders, sprayers, rakes and multifarious agricultural machinery and equipment were neatly assembled in rows in the field below me. A roup! I pulled over and got out of my car so as to get a better look at the items which would be up for grabs in the auction farm sale (roup) which the poster nailed to the gate announced as taking place the next day. Two immaculate John Deere combine harvesters, almost new and gleaming in their distinctive green livery with prancing stag logo, immediately caught my attention. I knew just who would be interested in those. I jumped back into my car and headed straight for Harry Barclay's house.

Harry was a country lad. With little education he left school at fourteen and followed the family's Scottish farming tradition. He grew his business until he owned farmland all over Britain and more than sixty substantial companies. He was a millionaire many times over.

I had met Harry after buying a house in the same country town where he lived. He took something of a shine to me as a young hopeful making my way in business and in due course, as with all his close friends, I was allowed to walk in unannounced to his home and to his kitchen - Harry ran his entire business empire from there. So when I arrived at his house I did just that.

Harry, in open-necked shirt as always, was seated at the kitchen table when I entered, head down studying papers and telephone to hand. He neither looked up nor said anything. I boiled the kettle, made us each a mug of tea, took them over to the table and sat down. Without ceremony I said, "There's two brand new combines for sale at the farm down the road. Thought you might be interested."

Without breaking from his work or looking up, he quickly shot back, "Sold them yesterday!" With that he went back to his cup of tea and on to his next telephone call. Matter dealt with. Concluded. And it was. Quick and simple.

Since then and throughout my life I have endeavoured to model what I am and my way of working on Harry. I have concentrated on developing an attitude of mind which cuts out all the peripheral 'bull' and sticks to the simple issues. Why? I'll tell you why. Let's look at what happened in the scenario I've just recounted.

The first thing to note is that Harry already knew all about the roup and the particulars of it. Of course he did, he was the master of his industry. It was his business to know everybody in it and to know everything that was going on. How foolish of me as a wet behind the ears greenhorn not to realise that!

The second thing to note is what Harry said; he said, "*Sold* them yesterday." He didn't say, "*Bought* them." He said, "*Sold* them." The reason for my emphasis of what he said and my repetition is that this is one of the two most critical lessons to success in business that I ever learned (the other was to use the power of my subconscious). It is therefore the most valuable piece of learning for you also. Here it is -

Successful entrepreneurs never buy then sell, they first sell and then buy!

The simple sense of the sell then buy philosophy is so powerful that it totally goes over the head of the majority of the populace. If presented to them most will question how it can be. Surely you must buy something before you can sell it? Not so.

Harry's 'sold them yesterday' response told me that his wide knowledge of the industry, what was going on and the people within it, meant that he always knew who was in the market and for what. So, long before this roup came around, he knew -

All the machinery and equipment which would be on sale
and
Buyers who were looking for them

Harry contacted those buyers and sold them the combine harvesters. Then he contacted the auction company and agreed the purchase. The machines would not come up for sale on the day of the roup, they'd be passed by as 'withdrawn from sale'.

Harry had taught me the priceless lesson that, to succeed in business, you must first sell before you buy it. In that way you need never make a loss. Nor will you ever have cash tied up holding stock; nor ever need financing. Simple and brilliant! So simple in fact that the majority of people cannot see or will not believe that such a practice lies at the very heart of the success and huge wealth of those such as Harry.

Harry also sold only at top dollar and bought only at bottom dollar. His purchases came exclusively from roups, bankrupt and distressed sales. The many farms, prime farmland and stock he owned all over Britain, he only ever bought from the banks who had repossessed them. They came to him at 'debt only' cost.

POWER POINT - *"Buy only at absolute rock bottom dollar."*

Harry's success made him both popular and unpopular in equal measure. Many in the farming community saw him as a vulture feeding of the carrion of other farmers' failures. Others saw in him a guardian angel; one who rescued farms, and often whole communities, from ruthless developers and asset strippers. And he was indeed a generous man.

Although he would not help out a failing business (he'd wait until it went bust), he would give assistance to those ousted from their farms and often re-employed them as operations managers. As such they retained the roof over their heads, management of the practical aspects of their farm and enjoyed a regular wage. They only lost financial control. Harry and his specialist team assumed management and responsibility for the commercial aspects of the business. A win-win situation.

POWER POINT - *"Be ruthless in business but generous in life."*

Chapter 41

HOW TO WIN IN BUSINESS

The title of this chapter, 'How To Win In Business', implies that being in business is a competitive pursuit. It is! Make no mistake, it is a tough world, cut-throat even. No place for the faint-hearted. But don't fret. It's not all blood and guts. You can compete without coming into direct conflict with others. Here's how.

* **First** remember that your biggest enemy is ... yourself! Overcoming that adversary is your biggest challenge. Win that battle and you'll win the war too. How come?

Well, it's all about being your best self in a business context. You must aim to be the best in the business. When you become that, in every respect, then your business will be the leader in it's field, the one the others are chasing. To get ahead, and stay ahead, you must :

* **Know** the market. Learn everything there is to learn about the industry/market in which you are trading. Become a specialist and an authority on the subject. This will not only give you a head start on your competitors, they will also come to you for guidance!

* **Know** your place in the market and how to establish and improve it. Plan, prepare and execute your business with diligence. Every area of your business must be honed to perfection. That will include evaluating in depth some or all of the following disciplines, departments, activities and practices -

Accounting and financial management, legal and compliance, sales, manufacturing, operations, transportation, marketing and branding, personnel and human resources, purchasing, customer relations, communications and technology ... and more

- and taking appropriate action to make them efficient, effective and best in class.

* **Know** your competitors – inside out! Having looked inwards at the competitor who is yourself, you must look outwards at the competition in the wider market. The good news is that this need not be a 'direct contact sport'. Yes, it can be likened to a boxing match or an athletics race, but there's an easier way than indulging in the equivalent of physical confrontation. It's really rather simple.

What you do is to repeat the exercise of analysing and equating every aspect of your competitor's business in exactly the same way, and in the same detail, as you evaluated all the processes of your own business. In this way you can know your enemy even more intimately than he knows himself! Then you can lay your own plans and act accordingly.

So first look within. Then look with the same eyes outwith. Act on what you see. That is how to win in business.

POWER POINT - *"Look within, look outwith, act on what you see."*

One thing you should never do in business is speak badly of other businesses. Especially your direct competition and those working in the same field as yourself. Don't 'trash the competion'! Such an approach will succeed only in discrediting yourself. Why?

Firstly - In promoting your business, your focus must be on what you can do and what you do well, not on what someone else can't do or does badly.

Secondly - It brings into question your own integrity. If you are seen and heard to speak badly of a third party, what might you be saying to others about the person or client you are addressing your remarks to?

Thirdly - It is negative behaviour and will be recognised as such. People do not do business with negative individuals. They respond to upbeat and positive overtures.

Fourthly - When your opposition are lacking in certain aspects of their business or comportment then a savvy client will find out anyway. Let the source of the 'bad news' be someone other than yourself.

Even if the client brings up himself failings or shortcomings in a competitor and asks for your verification, view or opinion on the matter do not get sucked into vilifying them. Apart from other considerations you could be guilty of defamation. That aside, it is best that you sidestep any criticisms of your opposition. Better by far to say something nice or complimentary about them instead; that will earn you respect.

At the very least, do not comment. Restrict conversation to the industry in general and redirect it towards the benefits which you and your enterprise have to offer.

Your client will soon come to realise that your greatest selling point is that you are a person of integrity. One to be trusted and one whose discretion can be relied upon. He'll know you and like you for it.

POWER POINT - *"Don't trash the competition. Focus on, and speak about, what you do well."*

Chapter 42

THE SHELF LIFE PRINCIPLE

Among the myriad of factors you need to be aware of in order to be an effective business practitioner, one of the most significant is what I call 'the Shelf Life principle'. This basically lays down that everything that you do and everyone that you deal with has a limited time span within which they are fully effective and/or of maximum value. When that time has passed then they must be discarded and/or replaced. So it's critical for the success of your enterprise to :

•Know when that time is imminent

and

•Act decisively without fear or favour

The optimum period of time in question will of course vary from just a few weeks in some instances to many, many years in others. As regards employees for instance, I have parted company with more than just a few within hours, days or weeks, many after only a year or two. But others of genuine commitment and value to myself or my enterprises were with me throughout my career. The crucial thing is to be able to differentiate between quality worth persevering with and those whose futures would be better catered for elsewhere.

And the same applies as regards clients, contracts and projects. Some (hopefully all or many) will have shelf lives as long as your own professional life. But all need constant review and some will not be of benefit kept on board beyond a certain point, so they have to go. This itself is a policy of review and renewal and creates space for fresh, more appropriate opportunities to be pursued and to occupy your time and efforts.

There is also the question of growth. Expansion of your enterprise must not come at the cost of retaining unproductive personnel or unprofitable clientele whose presence is paid for by new and rewarding projects. Retaining bodies or contracts just to make up the numbers is never a good idea. Better to do without as regards staff until people of the right pedigree are available; and the same applies to enterprises which have outlived their usefulness.

So work your employees and your contracts to the maximum benefit of all, while you can. But be aware that people and circumstances change, not always for the better, and that a parting of ways will in many cases become inevitable. Remember, you're not in business to be liked, so bite the bullet and do the necessary.

Apart from trying to be just too damned likeable to those who you really need to rid yourself of, there are other reasons that can cause your business venture to fall by the wayside. The mistakes entrepreneurs make are mostly incredibly simple, so simple in fact that it may be hard to comprehend how anyone coming into business could possibly fall into the traps. But they do – all the time!

The two biggest failures are :

An inability to create sales

and

Poor money management

Yes, simple but true. Not getting enough cash coming in and failing to look after it properly when it does are the single biggest killers of fledgling businesses.

POWER POINT - *"Concentrate your efforts on sales and money management. Negligence of these are the biggest killers to businesses."*

These faults themselves derive fom one big failing on the part of the budding entrepreneur. And that is :

The lack of a properly assessed business plan with ongoing oversight and management.

Generally speaking, those entrepreneurs with good plans, soundly managed and regularly assessed, do not experience the lack of sales and money management difficulties which can prove to be terminal for many. There are though other common pitfalls. While I much prefer to concentrate on success and all the positive aspects of running a successful business, it would be remiss of me not to mention these :

Accountants and lawyers are not nearly the best sources of business advice. I make my view on this clear elsewhere.

Banks may or may not wish to lend you money. Either way I recommend that you avoid them. Starting a business with borrowed money is not my idea of fun.

Credit too should be a no-no. I describe later how to have your clients/customers finance your business.

Don't fool yourself with concepts and ideas for your business which you haven't properly qualified and backed up by hard facts, real attributes and a detailed explanation of all the steps in the business process and how they will function.

Elevator pitches are as seductive and misleading to yourself as they are to listeners. A short description of your idea, product or company delivered in a way that anyone can quickly understand is often used as a substitute for a real business plan. It's not.

Fatal flaw is to forget, neglect or plain not know to carry out a strategic analysis or external review of the environment in which your business will operate now and in the future. Without this you are just taking a blind leap of faith.

Go big on market research, it's money well spent. New and existing small businesses spend on average less than twenty percent of invested money on marketing. That's too little. Underestimating the importance of marketing is possibly the biggest single blunder you can make when coming into business. You must know about identification, selection and development of your product or service; determination of price; selection of distribution channels to reach the customer; development and implementation of a promotional strategy and branding. You must spend on these.

Hard to do are trade sales. They may be easy to say but if you don't have direct trade to trade sales experience and contacts within the industry/sector in which you are trading then you will struggle.

Important beyond words are relationships. Building them is a long term strategy but they create trust and trust leads to revenue. A long term and profitable business - isn't that what you want?

Chapter 43

A THOUGHT ON FREE SPEECH

We live in a time when free thought and free speech are becoming ever more suppressed; a time when headline electronic chatter seems to be the only form of 'discussion' and the sole source of personal opinions for many and when the expectation of society is that everyone should be equal in mediocrity. Yet this mass move towards mindless sameness creates fabulous opportunities for those prepared to defy the new convention, contradict popular opinion, work things out for themselves and express themselves without restraint.

Of course there's nothing new in this; it is just such independent thinkers who have always been at the forefront of all developments in society in every era. It is innovators and contrarians who create change and those who take control of their own destiny ultimately shape, not only their own lives, but the lives of all.

POWER POINT - *"Innovators and contrarians create change and shape destiny."*

So when you elect to become self-employed you are doing far more than just setting up a small business. You are choosing self-determination over enforced labour, freedom of thought over toeing the company line, the freedom to act as and when you see fit and to let your imagination run wild unconstrained by outside limitations. And more significant even than any of those things you are, whether you know it or not, stating loud and clear that you are your own man, setting your own standards and norms, that you refuse to be bound by convention and that you insist on your right to free thought and to free speech.

I've written elsewhere about the attempted suppression by groups in society of expressing yourself through satire and humour and the feeling among these people that ideas and opinions other than theirs are 'offensive'. Those people have no place in your life. So rid yourself of them. Those who are offended by your stance don't matter and those who matter in your life won't be offended. It's important that everyone speaks out about their right to free speech and that others stop being offended by it!

POWER POINT - *"Those who are offended by your humour don't matter and those who matter in your life won't be offended."*

Of course, side by side with rights, any rights, goes responsibilities. I often think that this point is not stressed sufficiently, if at all. Anyone demanding rights must also accept the responsibilities of the rights granted to them.

Abdication of responsibility should automatically entail a corresponding loss of entitlement. After all that is what will happen to you in your self-employed situation. If you don't look after your business properly then you can't expect to enjoy the benefits of a successful enterprise. It would be crazy to think otherwise!

You only have the right to the rewards if you exercise responsible management and create a profitable environment.

POWER POINT - *"With responsibility comes rights and vice versa. You cannot have one without the other."*

Responsible management includes exercising your right to freedom of expression thoughtfully. There are many things don't need saying and there are many things best left unsaid. So don't say them. Speak about your affairs little and then only to the few who truly empathise. There's no benefit to you or to the wider world in everyone knowing every tiny detail about you and how you conduct your life and business. By behaving discreetly, others will come to trust you. If a client (for example) never hears you talk of your other clients' affairs then he will be confident that you don't discuss his business with others.

So yes, hand in hand with the right to free speech goes the responsibility to behave well in the handling of your own and other people's private information ... confidentiality!

I've never quite worked out if I'm a private sort of guy because of the work I do or if it's the confidential nature of the work which has created my ultra secretive persona! The truth is probably a bit of each. Either way, there is no doubt that my personality is well suited to dealing with the personal affairs and the financial and commercial secrets of my clients.

Being discreet is not I believe a trait which should be restricted to just those in my line of work (business, finance and personal consultancy). Surely discretion and the ability to keep a secret should form an essential part of any person's character if they are to be regarded as ethical in their dealings and trustworthy? After all, a person's most prized possession is (or should be) their integrity. It's above value.

POWER POINT - *"Your integrity is your most valued possession. Guard it well."*

You shouldn't only be discreet with the personal and confidential information of clients, you must also protect your own integrity and that of your enterprise. You should, for example, keep close to your chest the inner workings, ideas and practices which give you a business edge. In just the same way as you wouldn't hand over the keys of your safe or the password to your bank account, you should give consideration to how much of your business you reveal (offline and online) and devolve to others, for example web designers. When you contract out to suppliers in situations such as theirs, they exercise great control over an essential area of your business. The knowledge that they can and will disrupt your business at their whim (a dispute regarding service provided and/or payments is a common scenario) explains exactly why I design and maintain my own web site(s) and on independent servers.

In the wider context, the principle of keeping control of your own resources and materials holds good in all areas of life and business.

Contracting out and employing is important of course, particularly so where you want to grow and expand your business. There is a limit to how much you can do yourself and how many skills you can master.

But you need to learn where to draw the line and at least understand that there is risk involved in devolving certain of your work to third parties. The trick is never to give away the keys to your operations; be that the physical keys to your safe or the pass keys to essential resources - such as your web site.

Ensure that you, and you alone, are the only person to ever have control of 'the keys' of your business and then no one will ever be able to steal your assets or hold you to ransom.

POWER POINT - *"Keep personal and sole control of the keys of your business – always."*

Chapter 44

RANDOM ACTS OF MINDLESS OPTIMISM

While I cannot over emphasise the importance of proper planning and preparation as essential cornerstones of great achievements, I must confess that a sizeable chunk of my own entrepreneurial success has, over the years, been down to what I term 'random acts of mindless optimism'.

In fact I'd go as far as to venture that these random acts of mindless optimism (often known as taking a flyer or diving in the deep end) play a major part in the success stories of most entrepreneurs, the tendency to act this way being a natural element in the entrepreneurial DNA.

As Rabbie Burns, Scotland's national bard, famously wrote - "The best laid schemes o' mice an' men gang aft agley." Bearing this in mind, is planning necessary or desirable in all circumstances? After all, no matter how meticulously a project is planned, accidents or misfortune can still befall it. By the same token but in reverse (reverse psychology), sometimes, just sometimes, acting quickly on impulse or gut feeling can pay handsome dividends.

POWER POINT - *"Grab opportunities. Acting on gut feeling often pay off handsomely."*

I have in the past indulged in too many such off the cuff adventures as is possible to list here, but suffice to say that a remarkable number of them involved totally chance encounters with complete strangers in far flung hostelries!

One such episode occurred one evening when I shared a pint with a guy I bumped into in a north of England bar. This chap was very successful in the art business, buying paintings from artists all over the country and importing them from abroad too. He then sold them on at considerable mark ups at exhibitions he arranged at various locations. He was in town to host just such an event the following day. Would I like to pop along?

The next morning, pop along to the art exhibition I did. Although a total greenhorn regarding art works and the business surrounding them, I was very impressed by what I saw. The promoter was doing a roaring trade. In conversation with him it turned out that he was not in good health and struggling to maintain his workload. I sensed an opportunity.

Before the day was out I had bought his business, his entire stock and the names of all his artists and suppliers (one a Hong Kong art factory). I rebranded the business as 'Old Master Paintings' and went on to enjoy massive success. I recognised a potentially lucrative but under developed side of the business in original oil paintings painted to order, so I majored on that to great effect. I moved the business on at a huge profit five years later.

The point is that, neither in this instance nor in many others, was I looking for the specific opportunity which presented itself. Often I had never met the individual(s) previously, had I the slightest inkling about the business(es) in question or how to operate them and therefore never had any plan or strategy in place regarding them. In all cases I acted impulsively and without rational forethought; my on the spot commitments comprising much wishful thinking and being nothing more than random acts of mindless optimism.

But the fact that many such rolls of the dice had successful outcomes act as an important reminder that, just as misfortune can befall a well planned project, good fortune can embrace an unplanned one!

POWER POINT - *"Good fortune can embrace an unplanned project."*

So, having whetted your appetite as to what is possible when you employ my various guidelines of the preceding chapters and adopt a 'random acts' mindset, I invite you to move on to the third section of this book.

There you will learn how to establish a new business from scratch at zero cost; acquire an existing business at zero cost; and run any business at absolutely zero cost.

It's what I call – mastering the art of working smart!

BOOK 3

YES YOU CAN – ABSOLUTELY FREE!

How To Win Big At Zero Cost

Joseph T.Riach

Chapter 45

EVERYTHING FROM NOTHING

It amused me to read an article recently which was entitled, "Can you really set up and run a profitable marketing business for just ten dollars a month?" Why my amusement? Because I know that it's more than just possible to do – I assert that it's both easy and, from an entrepreneurial viewpoint, essential to do so. Not only with some minor internet marketing activity but with meaningful, real world, 'bricks and mortar' businesses. I know, I've started many substantial commercial entities from *absolutely nothing*. I've also made them *self-financing* and in need of *zero investment* from day one.

POWER POINT - *"Strive to create the most from the least."*

Surely the very essence of entrepreneurship is to create the most from the least? Anyone not using their initiative and ingenuity to that end hardly qualifies as an entrepreneur in my book. I made it my purpose to get everything I could for the least cost possible; and that included businesses, companies and enterprises of all kinds. In fact I made an art form of the practice.

So successful was I, that I soon realised that there was never any requirement for me to pay to purchase or set up a business. Some people even gave them to me! Hence my amusement regarding the opening article headline. Never mind ten dollars, I wouldn't pay ten cents for a business. There is no need to.

There are those pieces of business, lucrative deals, contracts and the like which just seem to appear from nowhere, they drop into your back pocket as you saunter along the road. But you can't sit around just hoping this will happen. It won't. It only happens when you are already out there in the thick of things making or having made huge efforts, casting your net all around. Then sometimes, just sometimes, a completely unexpected bonus will arrive as if from nowhere.

My First Free Business

I started my very first enterprise at just twenty-three years of age. Up to that point in time I had harboured just two ambitions in life. One was to be a professional footballer. The other was to be my own boss; from an early age I was determined to call the shots. I quickly understood that I was so opinionated and headstrong as to be unemployable anyway. So working for an employer was never going to be an option for me. As a teenager I fulfilled my first ambition but had my career as a professional sportsman cut short by injury. That's when I turned to self-employment.

I found a one man driving school business for sale with an asking price of five hundred pounds sterling. The proprietor offered to put me through the driving instructors' certification course as part of the deal. I didn't have the money needed to make the purchase but discovered in conversation with the owner that he needed to sell quickly in order to look after his sick wife. I offered him seven hundred and twenty pounds, more than he had asked but based on twelve monthly payments of sixty pounds each. We settled on nine hundred and sixty pounds paid the same way. Thus I acquired my first business at *zero cost*, effectively *paid for by the seller himself* from his own tuition fees from the clientèle he had created!

The school came complete with a smart car (so I had *'free' personal transport*) and a book of existing clients. Most took a lesson once per week and all paid in cash. I delightedly pocketed the money, kept scant records and enjoyed a party lifestyle – for a year. Then I was summonsed to appear before Her Majesty's Inspector of Taxes. A sobering experience.

Lesson learned, I quickly set to establishing and keeping proper book-keeping, banking and money management systems. As I had attended grammar school I was both literate and numerate. I had actually excelled in languages, maths and arithmetic, so performing these administrative operations proved easy for me. They were less easy however for many other self-employed people and one man businesses!

My Second Free Business

As news of my ability in those areas spread, I found myself approached by other driving instructors, taxi operators, couriers and delivery drivers to keep their books for them and advise them regarding their dealings with 'the tax man'. Very quickly I had a second full time business operating. It had *not cost me a dime to set up and run.* It marked the start of my career as a serial entrepreneur, my love affair with being in business and cemented my fascination with how to acquire and establish enterprises for *zero cost.*

In time, the book-keeping service developed into a full blown accountancy firm. I employed fully chartered and certified accountants, book-keepers and assistants, seven in total. All were *paid in arrears on performance*, no up front wages or salaries. This, by the way, is the only way to employ people. If you as an entrepreneur are prepared to take the risk of earning far more than you could in an employed situation, then it's wise to work only with people of the same mindset; those prepared to earn more than the norm but on a 'when you get paid they get paid' basis. That way *you avoid up front outlay*. You'll never be out of pocket.

POWER POINT - *"Work only with people who accept payment as you do, on a performance only basis."*

Soon I discovered that accountancy was the gateway into every aspect of clients' businesses as well as their personal affairs. So I set up a separate business consultancy.

My Third Free Business

The consultancy became my main 'baby'. I enjoyed passing on my own experiences in business and, being an imaginative individual, devising solutions to clients' situations which were innovative and not main stream. In due course the enterprises and projects I became involved in grew in number, scope and complexity, so I devoted considerable time to night school classes and residential courses, gaining appropriate qualifications and certifications. I regarded myself (still do) as what I call 'a hands on' consultant as opposed to a 'blue chip' one.

This because my modus operandi is to go into a client's business, work there for a period of time as necessary and see first hand how things operate and from there conceive solutions. This as opposed to being a 'learned it from a book at college' type who has never seen or experienced the inside workings of a real business. That, and the fact that I had by now personal experience in running my own diverse range of businesses, made me an increasingly sought after contract executive.

My philosophy as regards accepting commissions was never to say "no" or "can't do". I frequently put myself in the position of taking on a project and then having to frantically scramble to work out how to do it. But passing up on an opportunity has never been in my nature.

POWER POINT - *"Don't pass up on opportunities. Just say 'Yes'!"*

I sought help too of course. As the consultancy grew, I contracted specialists (on the same *performance/reward basis* as before mentioned) in the areas of computers, technology, communications, marketing, import, export, manufacturing, transportation and many other required disciplines. I was the generalist, the face of the business – and the sales specialist.

I had concluded quite early on that, no matter the business, the area, the discipline, the goods or services you're involved in, all are irrelevant if you can't sell them. Making or having the finest product in the world is useless if you can't sell it.

POWER POINT - *"Sell! The finest product or service is useless unless you can sell it."*

So I made my priority selling. I worked hard, trained, studied and practised to become the best of the best in the

---

selling business. I succeeded. But I had assistance and a proverbial chance encounter helped too.

My Fourth Free Business

I bumped into an acquaintance from my footballing days who was a banker. He had recently taken over a regional management position with a major London merchant bank. He asked if I might introduce him to some of my clients. For those he did business with he offered to pay me a commission. I knew this fellow well by repute and trusted both him and the bank he represented. I agreed to his proposal.

In due course he was receiving a trickle of my clients and fixing them up with secure bank accounts, savings schemes, insurances, pensions and investments. I in return received a cheque from him ... then another, then another. They were not insignificant amounts. That, plus the fact that my clients were all mighty pleased with the arrangements, led me to introduce more of my clients to him. The cheques kept coming. So much so that I started to wonder, "If he is paying this much to me, how much is he and the bank making?"

My thinking had long been to keep everything in the business in-house. This way I could 'keep control' of my clients by providing every service they might need. I had learned in my early days the folly of losing grip of your clientèle to outside agencies (accountants and lawyers for example) who then persuaded clients to do business with them or introduced them to their own favoured sources. I had no such fear with my banker friend but I was keen to look into how I might provide these financial services myself within my accountancy/business consultancy company. So I paid him a visit.

He was absolutely delighted to see me and immediately agreed that I should become a freelance agent to the bank. The only obstacles were that I first had to be invited by the bank to join them (they did not employ by application) and secondly, I had to gain appropriate qualifications to allow me to trade in the various banking, investment, derivative, pension and insurance products. The invitation, based on the reputation I had established in my consultancy business, was soon forthcoming and then it was back to school for me. I soon found that, the product and licensing education apart, the company placed a high premium on proper, professional selling and provided the finest training in that regard imaginable. Better still!

I urge all aspiring business people, and even those who are already experienced professionals, to work, train and study to be the very best sales person that you can possibly be. Doing so will not just make you a more successful, wealthier sales or business person. Doing so will raise to unimaginable heights your own self-esteem and the regard in which others hold you.

POWER POINT - *"Work to be the best sales person ever. It will pay you handsomely."*

Best of all, my education and training with the bank *didn't cost me a single cent.* Nor did I incur any cost representing them. *They paid for everything*; business expenses, travel, accommodation and entertaining. They even *provided me with an office and a personal assistant.* This meant that I could *run all my other businesses at the bank's expense.* This they were happy to do ... provided I pulled in the business for them. I set about doing that with a vengeance.

As I now had available an entire range of quality investment and financial service products in-house, I provided for my clients a complete suite of inter-related business and personal consultancy services and products. I offered friendship, trust, confidentiality, quality service and simplicity - a complete cradle to grave solution! My clients were captive but happy in the knowledge that their every need was catered for and they had no need to look elsewhere. I, in turn, had *no need to find clients 'cold'* (that bane of salespeople's lives), I already had them lined up and warmed up within my existing accountancy and business consultancy set ups. It was perfect. In no time at all I became the leading provider of new business to the bank.

And *my entire operation and huge cash earner was set up absolutely from zilch. No cost whatsoever.*

My Fifth Free Business

The next thing I felt that I needed to supply for my clients was legal services. I was not at all impressed by the time it took lawyers and solicitors to deal with the work I needed of them (both for myself and my clients) and I was even less impressed by the quality of their work and the cost involved.

The last straw came when I drafted myself a six page franchise agreement for a project in which I was involved. I was very thorough in my work, covering every conceivable point and including in fine legalese lots of "in-the-event-of", "not-withstanding" and "wherein-as-before" type caveats!! Once it was completed I took the document along to a local lawyer to have it checked. He kept the document for six weeks, in spite of my daily calls and pleadings to have it returned, before eventually summoning me to his office to collect it. When I met with the lawyer he admitted to not having yet read it! - but did so in my presence.

After a thirty minute examination he declared it to be perfect, flawless – not a single alteration was recommended. I was then charged six hundred pounds sterling for the consultation (this is thirty years ago at the time of writing). That worked out at one hundred pounds and one week per page. He didn't even certify the document. But he did me a favour.

I now realised that I was more than capable of drawing up properly worded and binding legal documents myself. Not surprisingly I quickly resolved to write all of my own contracts from then forward and forego having them scrutinised by a law firm. Subsequently I produced contracts for my clients too and at a fraction of the cost charged by lawyers.

But I knew that I also needed lawyers in-house to attend to the many requirements of my clients. I also needed 'tame' ones; those who would do what I wanted, the way I wanted and when I wanted. In due course I recruited two excellent individuals. One was Iain Bruce (mentioned elsewhere in this book). He was something of a loose cannon to the legal establishment and therefore perfect for me and my business!

My Sixth Free Business

In the meantime, on the back of my success with the bank I represented, I was approached by a major insurance company to, first train their UK wide sales force according to my successful and innovative, 'non-selling', relationship building techniques and, secondly, to set up a regional sales office and operation for them in Scotland. The latter I undertook as a freelance agent (so that I owned the operation), again *at no cost to myself* and with *all expenses paid* by the company, and quickly established a successful sales force of twenty-two top professionals. After just two years my thriving operation was bought out by another substantial world wide insurer. Once again *I had created substantial profit from zero outlay.*

My Seventh Free Business

At this time I needed to expand my accountancy operation. I needed more staff and bigger premises. I found an accountancy practice which was for sale. The proprietor, a fully qualified lady (we'll call her Susan), employed two other accountants and three assistants. She owned the premises she operated from. It was a substantial former bank with secure vaults. It had more than enough space to accommodate both her own and my staff and all our accountancy operations. The reason she was selling was both intriguing and surprising.

Surprising because Susan was broke and in debt. Yes, even accountants can be poor money managers. Yet she was a fine professional, worked extremely hard and had an extensive book of quality clients. Her difficulty was that she gave too much of herself and asked for too little in return. She put in such long hours (including nights, weekends and holidays) satisfying her clients' every needs while being overly lenient with her pricing and lax with her payment collection, that she had run into debt and become quite ill because of it. With her health ailing, things only got worse. The debt and the stress piled up and her downward spiral accelerated. Susan needed out.

After several meetings and assessment of the situation, I made her an offer she didn't refuse. This was the deal.

I *paid Susan nothing for her business* but -

I set up a new limited company. The company traded as accountants and employed all her and my own existing staff. The company operated from her existing premise and paid her a rent for that. She managed the whole operation on a day to day basis, worked only normal office hours and earned a salary. She had no say in or control of company finances. Me and my team managed the money side.

All Susan's existing clients were contacted and informed that her existing business was closed. They were told that their accounts would be transferred to the new company. But first, those with outstanding debts to Susan's original accountancy firm, had to settle their debts to her in full. Second, they had to agree to a *monthly direct debit payment* system with the new company (this was the same as I already operated in all of my businesses).

POWER POINT - *"Make your business a pay up front one – or get into a business which is. No exceptions."*

When I first put those terms regarding payments to Susan she exclaimed, "You'll lose half my clients!" My response was a calm, "No. You'll lose all your bad payers!" In the event eighty percent of her clients transferred to the new company under the new terms. Of those who didn't transfer, all who were due her fees did pay up, either promptly or after having been taken to court.

The result was that Susan had been given a new life. She had an expanded business with more staff and more clients. She worked only nine to five, five days per week, earned a salary and enjoyed regular holidays. She received rent from the company for the use of the premises; the windfall income from the previously unpaid fees cleared her debt. She was a happy bunny … and became a healthy one too.

There were no bad payers. Quite the opposite in fact. Because of the monthly direct debit payment system, all clients *paid for the company's services in advance*. My clients created a *positive cash flow* from day one. They paid Susan's salary, the premise rental and every other business expense. *They financed the business!*

So I had successfully expanded my accountancy practice as I had hoped to and moved into bigger and better premises in the process. I had acquired a top quality accountancy operations manager and doubled my number of clients and the income from them.

And *I did it at – zero cost!*

My Eighth Free Business

Another example of setting up a second company in order to 'rescue' another came about with Alan.

Alan had constructed from scratch a thriving offshore fire and safety equipment supply company. With his success his status and self-assurance had grown and he was well known, liked and trusted in the 'oil industry scene'. But when he called to see me he was a nervous wreck.

It transpired that his reputation and the potential for future stock market listing of his company had placed his business firmly in the sights of venture capitalists. These entities usually seek out growing businesses of substance in order to invest in them and assist their growth until they are ready for stock market flotation. When a company 'goes public' in this way, it is traditionally a time when its value can rocket and both the original entrepreneur and the investors typically enjoy windfall profit from the flotation and a considerable return on their investment.

Alan had been approached by a venture capital company and he had done a deal with them. The future looked rosy. But things had not worked out as Alan had expected. Now, a year later, he was quite literally in despair and desperate for help.

Alan told me that he had expected that his company would receive financial input and management assistance to accelerate growth and, most significantly, specialist help to restructure the business and guide it to flotation. He had expected to continue to lead the company in the process. Instead he had found himself sidelined by venture company managers who had moved in and proceeded, in Alan's view, to undo his work and relationships with clients which he had painstakingly developed over many years. Alan was not being consulted in any of this and felt largely ignored.

Things had got so bad for him that he had become ill and had to take time away from his work. This had only made matters worse. When he had returned to his company after a few days of rest he found that he had been moved out of his office and relocated to a corner in the general office beside the cleaners' cupboard! That had proved to be the final straw. Alan told me that he no longer cared about a publicly listed company. He just wanted his business back and under his control as before.

I told him that that was not an option, it would never happen. But I did construct a solution. I suggested the twin company strategy. It was a variation of the plan I implemented when taking over Susan's accountancy business.

With Alan *meeting all the expenses involved* (warehouse, offices, transport, personnel etc.), I registered my own offshore fire and safety equipment supply company and opened for business. I signed an undated contract allowing Alan to purchase the company from me at any time up to three years forward at which time he was compelled to purchase it. Then I set about approaching all of Alan's original clients. All Alan had to do was pass me his company's client files and keep his head down for a couple of years until my company was firmly established.

It proved easier than I thought. The vast majority of Alan's clients were completely loyal to him and just as disenamoured by the new regime in his company as Alan was. As soon as their annual contracts with Alan's company expired, they renewed with 'me'. In less than eighteen months the majority of Alan's company's former contacts and contracts were in my company's pocket. Alan could now buy out my company but I advised him to wait a little longer. Then, two years to the day after first approaching me, he resigned from his own company and took over my one which was, to all effects and purposes, his original company as it had been before his ill fated liaison with the venture capitalists.

Once again, *I had created a substantial business and profit from absolutely zero.* Just as important in this case was to see the joy on Alan's face and his return to full health and the happy, relaxed individual he had been prior to the stressful events.

My Ninth And Tenth Free Businesses

When you are in the business consultancy profession, or working in any kind of professional advisory capacity, you need to be thick skinned. You must be able to separate yourself from the situation on which you are giving guidance. This is so for a number of reasons but primarily because clients, even those who have paid you vast fees, often do not follow your advice. It can be extremely frustrating to stand by and see them fail to do what you recommended.

Because of this I learned two essential strategies -

One was to always demand substantial *payment in advance*, I only ever accepted assignments on that basis. It was often said to me (again), "You must lose a lot of clients that way!" To which I would reply, "No. I lose all the big hassle and no pay clients!"

So, whatever business you are in, advisory or otherwise, work only for those who *pay you up front*. You'll increase your income that way, reduce your sleepless nights and, most importantly, find yourself dealing only with quality people on quality projects.

The second strategy I employed, usually in tandem with the 'Pay Up Front' one, was the 'Take Over' strategy. In this scenario I would agree to work with the client, not in an advisory role, but as a managing and operations director in full day to day control of the business. This meant quite literally taking over ownership of the company. Then I could implement my own advice without interference.

I organised this on a sale back basis. The *client signed the company or the business over to me at no cost.* In parallel with that I signed an undated sale of the company back to the client agreement, which he kept. This contract stipulated a sale price according to a defined financial equation and a maximum term of three years. Provided he came up with the cash the client could buy back his company at any time and at the expiry of three years he was compelled to do so.

I *acquired free of charge and sold (at substantial gain)* several major businesses in this way. Two of them came to me from existing clients and through tragic family circumstances.

The Murder Case

The first of these was a company supplying a unique service to the North Sea oil industry. Peter, a resourceful engineer and self-made man, had built up one of the most profitable businesses I have ever encountered. With a device of staggering simplicity he had created an exclusive niche and cornered the market. I had helped him grow his business which numbered in his client portfolio every meaningful oil exploration, oil recovery and oil service company in the world. Everyone who was anyone in the oil business utilised his company's services - and paid handsomely for the privilege.

Peter's brother was the sales manager for his company and travelled the world. On a trip to Germany he went missing. After several days of searching for him, police found his body locked in the boot of his hire car, ditched deep in a Bavarian forest. He had been murdered.

Peter was very close to his brother and absolutely devastated by the event. He was in no state to run his business and he felt that his twenty year old son was not yet ready to do so. As there was no-one else that he trusted, and I knew the commercial side of the business back to front, he asked me to take over until he felt mentally strong enough to return. I did so on the 'Up Front and Take Over' terms I described.

When, six months later, no progress appeared to have been made in tracking down his brother's murderer(s), Peter decided to go to Germany himself to find out what was going on. He stayed there interviewing witnesses and searching for clues for eighteen months. All to no avail. He returned from Germany but he was still not in a fit state to resume his business activities. I saw out the three year deal and sold his company back to him. By then Peter felt up to resuming his work but he was never quite the same man as before the murder.

The Motorcycle Crash

Walter's business was quite different. Not awash with 'oil money' like Peter's, but still profitable to a healthy degree, and operating in a quite different business sector. His company owned and operated a concrete factory. They manufactured paving slabs, lintels, cills and a host of other bespoke concrete products supplying the building industry. One morning I received a call from Walter's wife.

She told me that their son Paul had been involved in an accident with his motorcycle on his way to work at the factory that morning. Walter had rushed to the hospital to be by his son's side. As Paul was his dad's number two, that left no-one in charge at the works. So, with both of them at the hospital, could I go to the factory and keep an eye on things? By coincidence I had been due there to oversee a sales meeting with a major house builder that very morning. I high tailed it over there. Soon the news came through that Paul had died.

Just like Peter with his brother, Walter reacted very badly to his son's death. He just couldn't accept it. No way could he work and, in fact, he turned to drink. Once again I was in a position to help out. So I did so on my standard 'Up Front and Take Over' terms. The business continued to flourish under my control which encouraged Walter, having 'dried out' in the interim, to stay away and spend time with his wife for the full three years. At the end of the three years he was fit and happy to return.

As had been the case with Peter, my greatest satisfaction came from knowing that I had helped out a friend in a time of great need. It was satisfying indeed to achieve that and more so to see him return to work in good spirits. Of course I had once again, generated *considerable profit from absolutely nothing*.

My Eleventh Free Business

Peter's business, which I referred to in 'the Murder Case', involved, among other things, modifying shipping containers. His company didn't manufacture the large steel containers which you see stacked on quays and on the decks of the huge container ships which transport goods all around the world. He only made changes to them to suit his particular purpose.

One day during my tenure of Peter's company, I received an enquiry from a Norwegian source, asking to be quoted a price for the manufacture and supply of sixteen shipping containers. I checked with Peter to confirm that he was in no way interested in involvement with such work (which I knew his business was not equipped for anyway) and then responded to the same effect to the Norwegians. I added though that I myself might be able to help them out.

The result was that Obrecht, who owned the company, came to Scotland and I introduced him to a local shipping container manufacturer with whom I had, in the meantime, made a sales agency agreement. In due course a deal was done. The containers were manufactured to the high specification stipulated by Obrecht and to his complete satisfaction. They were delivered to his company in Oslo and I received a substantial commission. So was born my shipping container consultancy and supply agency. *It had not cost me a single cent!*

Obrecht and I became firm friends. I arranged and handled many similar transactions, both for him and for the many other industry contacts which he introduced me to.

He also introduced me to Käre.

My Twelfth Free Business

Käre created and manufactured his own range of natural ingredient cosmetics. They were very popular in Norway but he had no outlet for them in the UK. He offered me the main agency as importer and distributor in Britain. There was a substantial cost involved, mainly in buying stock, and complex import regulations.

I declined the deal and instead introduced Käre to a trader in the north of England called Nobby (yes that was his name). This guy was already in the import/export business and soon agreed to become Käre's agent for the whole UK. I then made a separate arrangement with Nobby to be his exclusive agent in Scotland. Nobby would supply me on a *'no sale, no pay'* basis, In other words he gave me stock, *I didn't pay for it.* I paid him only for what I sold after I had sold it. So I was in business, *once more at no cost to myself.*

Now I had to set up a sales operation. I decided to target hairdressers. There were, and still are, hundreds of such businesses in every city, town and village in the country. Those hairdressing businesses who became my agents were awarded an exclusive territory and won the right to sell an exclusive range of high quality cosmetics to their customers. As they bought and paid for their stock from me up front, my business (which had *cost me nothing*) was self supporting from day one with a *positive cash flow. My agents and their customers financed my business!* I even arranged for deliveries of my stock from Nobby to be made directly to my agents; thereby eliminating any need for stock handling, storage and attendant costs.

My Thirteenth Free Business

The notice read, "Contract Manager Wanted. Apply Within." I was standing outside the regional office of a major, national, building maintenance company and I was not reading the advert for the first time. It had been in place there for several weeks. I ventured inside.

'Short Ken' (referred to earlier) turned out be the area general manager and having trouble with a couple of major contracts. The clients were unhappy with the situation and Ken needed to sort things out fast. I volunteered my help short term as on site consultant, promising to resolve his difficulties and set up a permanent contract management solution for him. With no other solution on the horizon, Ken agreed. I knew nothing about the industry but set about learning straight away.

It proved to be a rough ride but, within six months, I had succeeded in bringing matters under control. I found an ex-army man, experienced in the industry, to become the permanent contract manager, *collected a substantial fee*, departed ... and was immediately approached by senior directors of the company to help them out trouble shooting in another part of the country. I continued to do operational consultancy work for them for three years. Afterwards I carried out similar assignments for several other companies operating in the same field, including lucrative overseas projects in Europe and the Middle East. All because I saw the ad for the contract manager, went in and proposed a solution!

My Fourteenth Free Business

Around the same time as I was involved with clients in the building maintenance sector, I visited an architect who had an office available to rent. One of my businesses needed the space. While I was there, he lamented the fact that his office was not as tidy as it might be because the company employed to do the daily cleaning were not performing well. I immediately told him that I had an office cleaning company (I didn't) and would happily undertake the work in exchange for the office space I'd called to see about. He agreed on the spot – *another free deal* - and I immediately got hold of some people from one of the building maintenance companies to help me out. They brought with them equipment from their own source and my contract cleaning company was born – *at zero cost of course.*

The architect had bought an unused church and had converted it into an upmarket gymnasium, spa and health club. It needed daily cleaning and janitorial services too. So my new business was awarded that contract. He also gave me the work of the initial cleaning of all the newly built houses on a large housing estate his firm was involved in and, from that, I won the job of doing the daily cleaning at the premises of the builder involved in the project. After only a year, my business was performing this service at offices and premises all over the country. Everything from entire tower blocks, to supermarkets, department stores, factories, airports and even work for the Ministry of Defence. The entire operation *never cost me a penny* and I sold it for a *big profit* many years later.

My Fifteenth Free Business

I became the first person in Scotland to have a pocket size mobile phone. How come? Well, in keeping with my good habit of daily scouring the classified advertisements of newspapers in order to keep abreast with what was going on in the world of commerce, I came across a notice from a technology company based in Manchester, England. They had developed a pocket size mobile phone. I gave them a call and arranged a visit.

When I got there I learned that they were indeed the very first manufacturer in the UK of a mobile phone which would fit in your pocket. Up until then mobiles had been restricted to being upmarket, in car items, operating via hefty equipment fitted in the boot (trunk) of the car. This company's new phone did indeed fit into your inside jacket pocket – but only just. It was bulky, very heavy and did nothing for the sartorial elegance of your tailored jacket. It was impressive nevertheless.

In little time I had arranged to become their sole agent for Scotland. *There was no cost involved.* They supplied me with a sample phone (mine to keep) and ancillary equipment (cables, charger, instructions, etc.). All were neatly packed into a black leather attaché case in much the same way as an assassin's gun parts are portrayed in films. All I had to do was find buyers and place the orders with the company, who then delivered the phones directly to them. I also set up a sales force and, in no time at all, we were selling the phones to practically every enquirer. They were an 'easy' sell.

Around the same time, cordless phones for use around the house were a hot item. But they were illegal in the UK. British Telecom still held a monopoly on telecommunication services and neither permitted nor sold them. My friend Nobby imported a container load of the cordless phones from Hong Kong. I persuaded him to supply me with them on the same basis as with the Norwegian cosmetics (*no upfront payment*).

As with the mobile phones the sale was straightforward – when done properly. The strategy was to place a cheap lineage, classified ad advertising 'a' phone for sale. The flood of enquirers, all hoping to get their hands on the item, clogged the phone line but all were visited and given a demonstration. Once the phone was fitted to their British Telecom line and they had made and received trial phone calls everywhere from the bottom of the garden, to the attic, to the basement and thirty yards up the road, there was no way they were going to have you disconnect it! I phoned in the orders to Nobby and he sent them straight out to the client. So, *absolutely no cost for me at all,* I only paid for phones after I, or one of my country-wide sales force, made a sale. And both my lines in telephone equipment, mobile phones and cordless phones, were selling like hot cakes. My company quickly became a leader in the field.

This business provided a classic example of how to spot an opportunity, maximise the return from it and *develop a serious enterprise from absolutely nothing.*

POWER POINT - *"Grab zero outlay opportunities and make them pay big time."*

I made a point never to discuss my business affairs with anyone or how I went about my business. Few people were aware of the extent of my activities or how I set up my *zero cost* initiatives.. There was no reason and no benefit to me in others knowing. Anonymity is best. On one occasion I was asked by the attendant at the filling station I used if I owned a particular enterprise which, in fact, I did not own. I drew her close to me and in a conspiratorial manner whispered, "Don't tell anyone." Neither should you.

Conclusion

With these numerous real life examples (and there are more) of my business exploits you can see that, not only is it unwise to pay to purchase or set up a business, it is unnecessary. With someone else incurring the cost or with payment arranged in an imaginative way, you can acquire, possess and/or operate just about any business you wish *absolutely free.*

As I've demonstrated, the opportunities abound. They are everywhere You need only be alert and on constant watch for them, ready to seize them when they arise. There are just two guiding principles you must employ -

* Ask for what you want

and

* Deliver on what you promise

When you follow those rules you will find yourself winning big in life and business – absolutely free and forever!

Chapter 46

A LOW COST HUGE PROFIT BUSINESS

Here's the run down on how to instantly create an amazingly *low cost huge profit business* from scratch. Over the years I have successfully employed several variations of the following model.

This is a summary of an actual project.

It cost me *practically zero to start* - just a few pounds, the cost of a few cheap lineage ads.

* **I placed** a cheap classified ad to run once each week on the 'business day' in the Business Services column of the local newspaper – "Secretarial Staff Services have qualified PAs available now - interim, contract, permanent."

* **I also** canvassed this service by mail and telephone to local companies found in all the usual business directories.

* **I placed** another simple and cheap classified ad to run for seven days in the Situations Vacant column of the local newspaper - "PA wanted."

* **I received** 27 replies to this ad, 16 were well qualified personnel, the rest less so.

* **I interviewed** 6 applicants and employed 1.

* **To the other** 15 well qualified applicants I offered a free job finder service to source interim, contract or permanent employment for them. All 15 enrolled.

* **These PAs** were sent, as appropriate by qualification and experience, to companies requesting the staff agency services as promoted in the first ad mentioned at the top of this report. Clients paid in advance for this service, *thereby funding my business.*

* **The entire** operation was managed by the one PA I had employed (work from home, payed on a commission and reward basis).

* **In the** following twelve month period 7 of the 15 PAs were placed in permanent employment (fee 10% of first year salary – *paid on appointment*).

* **The 8 other** PAs were placed in various temporary positions (15% fee) throughout the year with 2 of those transferring to permanent later *(my fees collected monthly in advance).*

* **The core** of 6 PAs first interviewed were retained and used frequently for quality temporary positions both during and beyond the original twelve months cited in this report, working both in-house for clients or remote from home.

* **My outlay** – time, finance, expertise - minimal. My income - substantial, many hundreds of % over outlay.

* **Plus**, *many other opportunities in different business sectors were identified through the contacts developed and a significant number of these were subsequently commercially exploited, producing very substantial profits.*

* **This model** can be applied to any trade, profession, business sector, online or real world (or combo). It's *easy, self-financing and lucrative.*

In this real example I simply set myself up as an employment agent, a middle man matching client companies with PAs and vice versa. In a short time I had a full blown business on my hands. I had no previous experience of the sector but I and my company became specialists in the field And, guess what? The secretarial service dove-tailed with my other activities and each fed clients and earning opportunities to the others. There was a snowball effect. So believe me, a heck of a lot can be generated from *zero outlay!*

As I said at the start of this section, I find it amusing that anyone would ask if it's possible to set up and run a profitable business for just ten dollars a month when, as I've shown, there are numerous ways to get into business at *no cost at all.* To do so you need only *your own initiative and the will to do it.* When you apply those anything is possible.

Chapter 47

INVESTMENT FRENZY

I am including this chapter about investment frenzy because of the crypto currency craze of recent times and to highlight the danger of getting swept up in the mania of it and similar schemes. It is not included because I see investing in crypto currency as an opportunity to make something from nothing. Quite the reverse in fact. I am including my thoughts on the subject in order to make clear to you that this is one type of risk I do not consider it to be worth taking. My views may not earn you money but, if you share them and act accordingly, they will certainly save you some.

Note : I have reproduced below my views on crypto currency investing as expressed in my three articles titled "Celebrity Investor Crypto Currency Enthusiasm", "The Crypto Currency Freedom Myth" and "Smoke And Mirrors, The Emperor's New Clothes" which were originally published on my blog site at ibosocial.com/wakeup2wealth on the 26th of September and the 18th of December 2017 respectively. On the latter date BitCoin, the benchmark crypto currency, was in the ascendancy and trading at around $18,000. It peaked at about $20,000 shortly afterwards. At the time of writing, 27th February 2019, BitCoin is trading at just $3,345 - and thereby vindicating my expressed view.

So should you invest in crypto currency? That's up to you. For me it's an emphatic, "No!" Why do I say that? There are several reasons. First off, if you need to ask the question then you shouldn't do it. A classic example of the answer being in the question! But there are several other more specific reasons to avoid getting flattened in the stampede.

The California gold rush of 1849 was just such a stampede and a handful of the early arrivals did indeed make fortunes. But the vast bulk of the prospectors found only pain and misery. A more recent example of the same phenomenon, but in the modern electronic age, occurred in the Dot Com revolution of the late nineteen nineties. So, in general terms, there is a full history of real experiences to learn from – and the lesson is that you're a great deal more likely to get burned by crypto currency than get rich from it.

I'm reminded of the story of the business executive who approached the landlord of a remote inn and informed him that the president of his company would be arriving later that evening with some colleagues to celebrate the winning of a lucrative deal. He assured the landlord that his boss would be no difficulty at all but that he did have one rather strange foible - he believed that beer bottle tops were money and would insist on paying for everything with them. So, to avoid any trouble, the executive advised the landlord just to accept the bottle tops and keep them for him and he would come to settle up the bill in the morning.

The master of the house agreed to the arrangement and the company president and friends duly arrived, enjoyed a riotous evening and ran up a considerable bill. The president paid for it all in bottle tops. The next morning, the executive arrived back at the inn and mine host reported to him that the company president had indeed visited and had run up a bill of thirteen thousand pounds. He produced the bottle tops to prove it. "Let's square up," he asked. "No problem," replied the executive, "Thirteen thousand pounds? .... let me see .... have you got change of a dustbin lid?!"

Humourous? Yes. Yet not difficult to see why crypto currency investing, as with previous purely speculative crazes, might be seen as on a par with bottle tops and dustbin lids. There's nothing of value there!

Smoke And Mirrors, The Emperor's New Clothes

Smoke and mirrors is an idiom for a deceptive, fraudulent or insubstantial explanation or description. The source of the expression is based on magicians' illusions, where they make objects appear or disappear by extending or retracting mirrors amid a distracting burst of smoke. The bigger the distraction the more complex the trick that can be accomplished. Complicating what is apparently before you is another way of cloaking what is really happening.

POWER POINT - *"Complication can deceive. A dustbin lid is a dustbin lid regardless of what you call it."*

The ultimate deception of all time was possibly that penned by Hans Christian Andersen in his classic tale of "The Emperor's New Clothes" in which swindlers persuade the emperor to buy a non-existent outfit on the basis that it is invisible only to fools. Not wishing to appear foolish, the emperor purchases the non-existent clothes and parades himself in public totally naked!

Is this the equivalent of what crypto-currency investors are indulging in? There is nothing new after all in people rushing like rabid dogs to get on the bandwagon of the latest sure-fire, huge profit scheme only to find that the bandwagon is already leaving town and the serious professional insiders who drove the price up have already jumped ship and cashed in big time. But not before preparing their life raft! In this instance in the form of creating a futures market and buying heavily into put options from which to gain even more prolifically from the falling price they've created by their exit than they did on the surging upward value which they had first manufactured.

You see, when all is said and done, phenomena such as the current crypto currency frenzy are created by shrewd operators fully conversant with the sheep mentality of the general public and the fear (of loss) and greed (for profit) emotions which drive them. The professionals know that they can blind and baffle their prey with smoke and mirror strategies and with ever more in-depth, intellectual, technical and apparently meaningful detail, repeated and proliferated by knowing (and unknowing) lackeys, well known people and celebrities. They confuse and confound the populace in similar fashion as was the emperor duped into believing that something not there was there.

But at the end of the day, one thing and one thing only powers the price of crypto currencies – the markets! Driven solely by speculation, backed by nothing, is investing in crypto-currencies the ultimate mugs game?

Celebrity Entrepreneur Crypto Currency Enthusiasm

There is a great deal of celebrity entrepreneur crypto currency enthusiasm around. Big wheels such as Richard Branson are happy to proclaim their investment and talk of their confidence in a positive future for the 'currency'. But, as such, there are points to bear in mind.

Branson and those like him have high public profiles, they tend to be seen, heard and listened to. Their entrepreneurial successes are well documented. When they say that a certain investment is a good one then the general public are likely to believe them and to follow their lead.

But the fact that Branson himself is an investor, and a substantial one, means that he stands to gain from promoting positive vibes in the market. He's using his influence to hopefully increase crypto currency value. He's talking up his own investment! ... and he knows it. He's a shrewd operator.

And although he's investing only a micro fraction of his total wealth in crypto currency it still is, to your average punter, a massive amount. But it's money Branson can afford to lose. He knows that crypto currency investing is highly speculative, so he stands to make considerable gain. But if it all goes pear shaped then he'll lose only the limited amount which he is quite prepared to wave goodbye to anyway. Besides, he knows how to and can afford to, hedge his bets (make money when the market falls). Smaller investors may not enjoy that luxury.

The reality is that these celebrity investors are no better able to forecast the future as regards crypto currencies than the next man. But they can influence the market in their favour and can therefore afford to speculate at much lesser risk than the man in the street. Here are a couple of points to ponder :

• Crypto Currencies in your portfolio are an investment; an investment with no underpinning asset. They are not cash.

• They are a purely capital investment. They generate and pay no income (unless a hybrid scheme)

• They fall into the Highly Speculative category

• As such you should invest only a very small part of your total investment kitty

• You should invest only as much money as you are prepared to and can afford to lose

• The value of investments can fall as well as rise.

• The value of highly speculative investments can plummet as well as rocket!

• Participating in a collective scheme of any kind usually incurs costs (hidden or otherwise)

• The more complex the collective or hybrid scheme the greater the dangers of all kinds – including fraud

• Governments are already taking interest – they'll want, and will certainly get, control and their 'pound of flesh'

Now, my observation of life in general is that these principles mentioned hold good in all times, rarely change and always repeat. From the Klondike rush to the Dot Com revolution, sub prime mortgages, you name it. There comes always a day of reckoning. And in all investment markets and cycles it is the small guy - that's you, not Branson - who, one way or another, picks up the tab at the end of that day!

Crypto Currency Freedom Myth

Many people are of the view that crypto currencies are the latest answer to escaping from governments and the state run central banks of most countries around the world. If only …

I had been invited to meet with a government treasury department junior official over a lobster and champagne lunch at London's famous Savoy Hotel restaurant. His brief was to elicit my independent views regarding crypto currencies and how governments and central banks might best get both involved and take control. He suggested that I prepare a review and report back to him in three months time. A hefty fee was mentioned.

But I quickly informed him that neither the time nor the report would be necessary and, drawing his white table napkin to me, I took my pen and started to scribble on it. This is what I wrote -

1. Government sets up their own crypto currency, let's call it BitDollars.

2. Government pays all public officials, employees, contractors and others only in BitDollars.

3. Government collects all taxes and inward payments of all kinds only in BitDollars.

4. Government outlaws/blacklists all other crypto currencies in much the same way as offshore tax havens are treated.

5. Government recruits/employs the finest blockchain technology specialists to evaluate all angles, progress suggestions, develop future technologies, monitor activity and police the system.

6. This is my fee ... I wrote a four digit number. Followed of course by - 'Cash only!'

Job done, I drained my champagne cocktail and left for the tranquility and calm of my happy home in the sunny south of

Portugal. The treasury department striped suit paid the lunch bill.

Conclusion : The fact is that governments/central banks may or may not choose to go crypto currency, they'll win either way. Crypto currency transactions are easily tracked and the people – you - who make them; crypto currency simply extends their fiat system from tangible to digital thus making it easier to take people's money. So crypto currencies extend the concept of the cashless society which 'the powers that be' want you to buy into so that they can control every aspect of you, your life and finances. It is, and increasingly will be, harshly controlled.

For those of you intent on being different and owning your own future, the so-called cashless society is the last thing you want. Participating simply plays into the hands of governments and authority. You should resist it at every turn.

Chapter 48

THE ART OF WORKING SMART

You should know by now that success in life or business is just not possible without the application of single minded determination and simple hard work. The two are essential to any meaningful degree of achievement. Yet, there is another trait which, when added to the mix, raises you to a different level altogether, makes you unbeatable. To truly succeed at the very highest level, you must - master the art of working smart!

POWER POINT - *"Work hard at working smart!"*

But what is working smart? What does it mean? Well, in my book there are three categories of work -

* Hard Work – Typically dealing with crises, pressing issues, deadlines, meetings and interruptions. Rushing around a lot and being very important.

* No Work – Attending to some mail, phone calls, popular activities, trivia, games and time wasters. Procrastinating.

and

*** Smart Work** - Smart workers spend time on Preparation, Planning, Prevention, Relationship Building, Personal Development, Enjoying Life – AND - they employ their Native Wit!

There are in fact two distinct aspects to *working smart :*

Native Wit and *Work Practices*

Of the two, native wit is natural and devastatingly effective. Most people who are employing it didn't learn it. They do it intuitively, it's part of their character, of who they are and how they were raised. Within this book, Harry Barclay is the perfect example. But you can aspire to be like Harry and others like him, both by -

* Altering the way you think, your attitudes

and

* Consciously applying appropriate life and work practices

To do so you'll need to give consideration to the following. No smart worker has all of them, but the more elements you manage to include into your working strategy and style, the smarter the worker you will become :

Put yourself first

Think before you act

Know what you want

Ask for what you want

Control your emotions

Be innovative and bold

Be in the right businesses

Look on the bright side of life

Know and play to your strengths

Employ good life management skills

Employ good time management skills

Identify and act on the right opportunities

Create intellectual products and/or services

Provide a scarce resource into a high demand market

Additionally you should -

Leverage other people's time and money

Hang out with only the best people

Know when to cut your losses

Keep things in perspective

Network and ask for help

Create and deliver value

Be nimble minded

Be Flexible

and

Be generous, compassionate and kind!

Working smart means finding your strengths and knowing your weaknesses as opposed to the doing it all yourself and burn out of working hard. It also means maintaining your personal integrity and never involving yourself in anything which diminishes you or goes against your personal values.

Above all else, working smart means knowing your self worth and never under selling yourself intellectually or financially.

POWER POINT - *"Value yourself highly, intellectually and financially."*

The idea of working smarter rather than working harder is not, of course, new. While it's easy to explain what working harder is – starting early, longer hours, staying late – it's far more difficult to define working smart. In the case of the Harry Barclay's of the world it is almost indefinable, it's an intangible entity, a state of mind, a way of thinking, a god given gift. However, one thing is certain. He and the others like him have an incredibly simple and intuitive way of seeing things or, to put it the other way around, they do not see or recognise complexity in anything. They blank out complexity and are the smarter for it. *They are astoundingly quick at seeing the obvious.*

POWER POINT - *"Keep everything simple. Blank out complexities. See what is in front of your eyes."*

While working hard entails much work, it is work which is not necessarily going to make a lot of difference. Smart work on the other hand makes a substantially bigger, and usually far speedier, impact.

To work smart :

1. Look at those things that actually move you forward in life. Separate out mundane tasks and delegate them to others.

2. Create disciplined but fun schedules with regular breaks. Do the hardest things first and early in the morning while your brain is fresh and alert.

3. Don't do tasks partially. Do it *now* completely or don't even start.

4. Be selective about doing only genuinely high pay off activities, plan them ahead and focus on them only at the point of involvement.

Remember too that enthusiasm should be tempered with wisdom. Consider beforehand, and at your leisure, all the details of whatever it is that you are contemplating so you can be sure that everything will be accomplished without fuss, on time and accurately.

5.   The importance of 'No'. There is no single ability which constitutes, and will contribute to, working smart on your part than saying "No" when you need to. Whether in personal life or in business, there is no benefit in taking on un-necessary work, allowing others to be unrealistic in their expectations of you or simply having people take advantage of your good nature. In order to dedicate yourself to the important aspects of your life and business you must know when to say, and be confident in saying, "No" to things which contribute nothing to your wellbeing or to the achievement of your objectives. Practice by saying "No" to as many people as possible, as often as possible. Do it just for the hell of it! You'll feel great. Saying 'no' is saying 'yes' to owning your own future.

POWER POINT - *"Saying 'no' is saying 'yes' to owning your own future."*

In reality, not just this chapter, but the entire content of this book is about working smart. All of the guidance, suggestions and examples are about urging you to do just that; to dare to be different, to own your own future, to think and work smart. The alternative is not appealing. It is to stay bogged down in the same rut as everyone else, as all those who are not daring to be different and are not determined to own their own futures. Where's the point or the excitement in that?

The main barrier to progressing as individuals and taking control of their lives which so many face is in their mindset, their attitude. When they encounter someone different to themselves, someone self-confident and in control, they become confused. They think that the difference is due to a freak of birth or some other cruel trick of nature to which they have been subjected. Therefore they look for the 'secrets' of the smart thinkers in ever more complex areas. Yet the very opposite is the truth. Those who work smart generally follow very simple life and business practices. So simple in fact that the majority of people cannot see or will not believe that these practices are at the very heart of the smart thinkers' success. Did you, for example, find anything complicated in my many absolutely free, everything for nothing, zero cost business projects?

POWER POINT - *"Working smart can produce absolutely free, everything for nothing, zero cost business projects."*

It's somewhat like the clue to the murder sitting on the mantelpiece. No-one expects it to be there, so no-one finds it. They search every nook and cranny, upturn every stone. To no avail. Yet all the time the answer is right there before their eyes. So with the art of working smart. It is simple activities carried out repetitively and well which mount up to great achievements. This is the single most powerful 'secret' of the smart worker!

POWER POINT - *"Simple activities carried out repetitively and well are what mount up to great achievements."*

But this is what so many cannot or will not see. And, before you can become a master of the art of working smart, it will be necessary for you to learn to think the way that smart thinkers do. This will usually involve a process of **uneducating** from your mind many well entrenched beliefs and practices.

POWER POINT - *"Learning to work smart will not be easy. Be prepared to uneducate yourself from thinking and working in complex ways."*

As very young children we mostly all display a high level of native wit. A range of natural thought processes and actions designed to allow us to live successfully in the wild. But modern society sanitises out much of this through our culture and education. So, by the time most people reach their twenties, they have totally capitulated to the expectations of society and to the peer pressure of the majority. They are thinking and acting just like the rest of the population who display, in all their thoughts and actions, a desperate desire to be equal in mediocrity. Don't let this be you!

Make it your aim to tap into the reservoir of native wit which still resides deep within you. Listen to your gut instinct. Work smart. Dare to be different. Own your own future. Win big in life and business!

CONCLUSION

A WORD FROM THE AUTHOR

Within these pages you will have found occasional repetition of texts. This is quite intentional. Important points receive more attention in this way. There are also included a few quotes from my other current publications - *Mastering the Art Of Making Money*, *Self-Improvement Should Be Fun!* and *The Simplest Sales Strategy*. This provides continuity across the series. I very much hope that you will read them all, benefit from the collective teachings and enjoy the overall experience.

As a writer it is not my intention that you should agree with all that I have to say. My aim is to provide you with alternatives and demonstrate to you that there exists other and, I believe, smarter ways to go about your life and business. If I only cause you to stop and ponder awhile, reflect on your life and give consideration to my guidance and my experience, then I will have succeeded in my mission. I will, in however small a way, have made an impact on your life and, hopefully, will have brought about improvement in both it and you.

I discovered a long time past that the surest way to achieve great things, personal satisfaction and wealth in my life was to concentrate my efforts on helping others, rather than on helping myself and focussing on material gain. Writing and telling others about my successes – and failures – makes it possible for me to spread this message to an audience of countless millions all around the world. This delights me beyond measure. It means that I can touch and, just maybe, help to improve the existences of an infinite number of people. There really can be no greater joy.

It's also the case that, although I have chosen not to write a biography in the classic sense, I have charted my life and revealed something of myself in what I have written throughout this and all of my books. I would like to think that this human aspect gives weight to my message and added encouragement; and to those close to me a reminder of the less than perfect but constant trier who acted out this marvelous adventure.

It's an adventure through which the following guiding principles became etched deep in my psyche :

* Your over-riding aim in life should be to achieve a state of tranquility and calm, an awareness of life's simple treasures and to feel constant gratitude for them.

* To fully appreciate life in that way, you must make kindness to others your priority.

* Through kindness and generosity to others, wealth in your commercial pursuits will find you.

* It is necessary to experience financial wealth in order to properly appreciate that it does not constitute, nor can it buy you, happiness.

* Once thus aware then you can put aside material ambition and achieve a state of tranquility and calm ....

.... and so the circle is complete.

Give thought to the following words adapted from the

letters attributed to Chief Seattle of the Suquamish and Duwamish native Americans (1786 – 1866) :

"There is no quiet place in the white man's cities. No place to listen to the leaves of spring or the rustle of insect wings; the clatter only seems to insult the ears. What is there to life if you cannot hear the lovely cry of the whippoorwill or the arguments of the frogs around a pond at night?

Neither do you seem to notice the air that you breathe. Like a man dying for many days, you are numb to the stench.

And what are you without the beasts? When all the beasts are gone, you will die from great loneliness of spirit, for whatever happens to the beast also happens to the man. All things are connected. Whatever befalls the earth befalls the sons of the earth.

This we know - earth does not belong to man, the man belongs to the earth."

What Chief Seattle foresaw was what he called the end of living and the beginning of survival. Today you can see the truth of his words, the evidence is all around you. War, famine, greed and pollution. More and more people are drawn into lives of mere survival rather than lives of joy and fulfillment. Don't let that be you.

You are an independent thinker, a contrarian. You are not the same as the others. You will win big in life and business because -

You dare to be different.

You own your own future.

You shout out loud and clear –

Yes I Can!

POWER POINTS

Every chapter of this book is based on my own real life experiences and each one contains what I consider to be valuable guidance as to how to most rewardingly conduct your life and business.

When studying such material it is not uncommon for readers to highlight points of particular significance to them or for future reference with, for example, a marker pen or by inserting a sticky note. In my previous books of the 'successful life and business' series – Mastering The Art Of Making Money, Self-Improvement Should Be Fun, The Simplest Sales Strategy (all of which I hope you read) – I made the highlights myself with my Power Points.

I did not originally plan to include such Power Points this time around but, such has been the clamour of approval for the strategy from readers, that I've relented. So I am once again summarising some of the essential messages from each chapter as my Power Points. I consider these points as critical to your success. Read them, memorise them, employ them. They will serve you well.

Yes You Can! – In Life

"Dare to be different. Being the same as others means at best being mediocre."

"Summon up the courage to defy convention and follow your own instincts and gut feelings."

"Generosity should flow from the heart and be enriching to

both donor and recipient."

"Say what you feel and do what you say."

"Swallowing your pride and asking for help takes courage. Not asking shows a lack of humility."

"You never know 'til a dead horse kicks you."

"Never underestimate the wisdom and wit of the common man."

"Striving each day to be the best that you can be is the best that you can be!"

"Small changes bring huge rewards."

"Choose to pursue your dream and do the thing you most enjoy."

"Make every day your best day."

"Tell yourself every day – 'Today is the best day of my life' – then go about making it so."

"Make time for physical exercise to sharpen your body – and mind!"

"Live a relaxed life to produce higher quality results and more of them."

"Snickling all day makes for fun, rest and play!"

"Trust your gut feelings, they will serve you well."

"To fully experience life, push yourself to your limit - and then a bit more."

"Do not assume responsibility for the envy and greed of those too lazy to create their own wealth."

"The pessimist sees difficulty in every opportunity; the optimist sees the opportunity in every difficulty."

"Great achievers share the common personality traits of vision, determination and self-belief."

"You are the richest man on earth – you just have to be smart enough to know it."

"What is lovely to one person is lousy to another. Perception of beauty is related to personal circumstance."

"What you put into life is what you'll get out."

"Your thoughts of today build your life of tomorrow."

"Life is not about perfection, enjoy what you have for as long as you have it."

"Don't let what you can't have spoil your enjoyment of what you do have."

"Everything comes to he who waits."

"If in doubt defer."

"Act on impulse, follow your gut instinct and enjoy a life of excitement, spontaneity and fun."

"Only some of your efforts will lead to success but all those ideas you don't act on will certainly fail."

"Use your smartphone selectively and only for constructive and appropriate tasks."

"Live life in the present moment by being present in your real life with the real people and things around you."

"The bulk of smartphone traffic is non-essential and access to it not an immediate requirement."

"Laughter starts at home – both physically within the family and personally within yourself."

"Laugh at yourself and grant others the right to laugh at and with you too."

"If I can laugh at you, you can laugh at me and we'll all laugh together!"

"Be exceptional, create only feel good days. Bad days are not acceptable."

"Kick the losers out of your life - and leave them out!"

"You already know within you what is right and what is wrong."

"Every day in every way I'm getting better and better!"

"The more I have fun, the more I get done!"

"I am kind and generous every day!"

"Today is my best day ever!"

"Always use upbeat, enthusiastic language. It's infectious. Everyone responds to it."

"Feed your integrity with positive thoughts and generous actions. Show your happiness to the world."

"Successful human beings accept sole responsibility for their own thoughts, actions and the consequences of them."

"Be true to yourself and earn the respect which your integrity merits."

"Only the present moment is real – relax and enjoy it."

"Implant positive beliefs in your inner psyche with repeated assertions of your strengths and achievements."

"Practice daily self critique and daily self love too. Be self aware."

"Have the courage to say what you think and show your true emotions."

"Create great relationships by recognising your own emotions and acknowledging other peoples'."

"When you shut down one emotion, you shut down them all."

"Struggling with and denying your emotions simply leads to more suffering."

"Ignoring or suppressing your emotions risks losing your identity and self-respect."

"Processing and experiencing your feelings is part of leading a full life."

"Why would you treat yourself with less care and affection than you would afford to a special friend or loved one?"

Yes You Can! - In Business

"Own your own future. Entrepreneurs beat the drum, they don't follow the band."

"Ignore others' worthless comments and go your own way."

"Never trust an 'expert'!"

"Only be being adventurous can you possibly gain."

"Entrepreneurs are leaders."

"Your passion and self-belief must be absolute in order to succeed in self-employment – or any area of life."

"Be a risk taker – and bold with it."

"Ask directly and spell out exactly what it is that you want from people and situations."

"Be focussed and unshakeable in your pursuit of excellence but flexible and resilient too."

"Laugh at yourself. Take your work seriously but never yourself. People don't like self-importance."

"You might have the finest goods or service on offer but unless you can sell them then you'll go nowhere – fast!"

"Whatever other business disciplines you may excel in, you will only reach your full potential when you master selling."

"Be prepared to have informed conversations with customers while displaying your in-depth, specialist knowledge."

"Being your own boss and having the duty of instilling motivation and discipline on yourself is harder by far than managing other people. Fail on this and your business fails."

"Everyone loves laughter and everyone loves you when you create laughter."

"There is education in school and college and there is education on the street. Seek out and master them both."

"The hard work in life or business is in the preparation."

"Trust your gut instinct. It will serve you well."

"Successful achievers possess and exercise relentless self-discipline."

"In life and business keep all things simple, work determinedly and avoid un-necessary expense."

"The more you have fun, the more you'll get done!"

"Choose to do only work which you truly enjoy and which helps other people."

"Let your passion determine your niche and then both will define your success."

"Try this and that; find your passion; establish your niche."

"To be the best, work only with the best."

"Compete by not competing. Think outside the box. Find innovative ways to get to clients first. Make an exclusive offer."

"Would you rather do business with someone pushy who you don't know or with someone trustworthy who you do know?"

"If you want higher self-esteem then find ways to boost someone else's self esteem."

"If you want to raise your positive spirit then assist someone else to raise theirs."

"If you want more happiness in life the smartest way to get it is to help someone else achieve it."

"Stand out from the crowd."

"The assertive and persistent succeed in business, the weak-willed fail."

"Do not assume risk or liability on someone else's behalf."

"Seek situations where the risk is minimal and/or shared and personal gain is substantial."

"You are not in business to be popular. Success comes from being respected."

"Be determined to persevere!"

"Successful entrepreneurs 'get on their bike' and speak to prospects and clients face to face."

"Do your market research and target your promotional work to the niche where your buyers are."

"Never think that success comes work free. Waiting for success is a long wait."

"You can prosper as an entrepreneur in any environment anywhere."

"A bad attitude is like a flat tyre. You won't get anywhere until you change it."

"Opportunity is seeing a solution to a difficulty."

"Do your selling yourself. You're the best person for it."

"Never let anyone have access to your cash."

"Better to employ no-one at all rather than someone you don't trust."

"Stand out from the crowd."

"Turn difficult situations into winning ones."

"Impress people with the simple excellence of your work."

"Reverse psychology – do or be the opposite of what people expect."

"Do not judge a book by its cover."

"Neither look up to the rich nor down on the poor."

"Perform – but perform as a better version of yourself."

"Presentation is everything!"

"Entrepeneurs are inventive risk takers who look for new ways to do things."

"Use loss leaders and incentivise customers with novel offers."

"Know your niche and develop your brand to appeal to it."

"Inventive entrepreneurs create their own market trends."

"Know everything about your industry, the people in it and all that is going on."

"Successful entrepreneurs never buy then sell, they first sell and then buy!"

"Buy only at absolute rock bottom dollar."

"Be ruthless in business but generous in life."

"You are your own biggest enemy – aim to be the best in the business."

"Know inside out your market, your place in the market and your competitors."

"Look within, look outwith, act on what you see."

"Don't trash the competition. Focus on, and speak about, what you do well."

"Act decisively to replace staff, clients and contracts when they become no longer useful, productive or profitable."

"Concentrate your efforts on sales and money management. Negligence of these are the biggest killers to businesses."

"Always work to a properly assessed business plan with ongoing oversight and management."

"Go big on market research, it's money well spent."

"Innovators and contrarians create change and shape destiny."

"Those who are offended by your humour don't matter and those who matter in your life won't be offended."

"With responsibility comes rights and vice versa. You cannot have one without the other."

"Your integrity is your most valued possession. Guard it well."

"Keep personal and sole control of the keys of your business – always."

"Grab opportunities. Acting impulsively on gut feeling can often pay off handsomely."

"Good fortune can embrace an unplanned project."

"Strive to create the most from the least."

"Work only with people who accept payment as you do, on a performance only basis."

"Don't pass up on opportunities. Just say 'Yes'!"

"Sell! The finest product or service is useless unless you can sell it."

"Work to be the best sales person ever. It will pay you handsomely."

"Make your business a pay up front one – or get into a business which is. No exceptions."

"Grab zero outlay opportunities and make them pay big time."

"Always ask for what you want and always deliver on what you promise."

"Complication is often a form of deception. A dustbin lid is a dustbin lid regardless of what you call it."

"Be true to yourself - live life, laugh and love."

"Work hard at working smart!"

"Value yourself highly, intellectually and financially."

"Keep life simple. Blank out complexities. Trust what you see."

"Saying 'no' is saying 'yes' to owning your own future."

"Working smart can produce absolutely free, everything for nothing, zero cost business projects."

"Simple activities carried out repetitively and well are what mount up to great achievements."

"Learning to work smart will not be easy. Be prepared to uneducate yourself from thinking and working in complex ways."

"Live to be different and to make a difference."

"Master the art of working smart."

"Dare to be different. Own your own future. Win big in life and business!"

RESOURCES

The resources referred to in this book are all valuable sources of information, inspiration and motivation which have proved to be of immense value to the author, everyone he works with and all those who he coaches in life and business skills.

Literature

Billy – *Pamela Stephenson*

Blowing the Doors Off – *Michael Caine*

Family Secrets – *John Bradshaw*

Homecoming – *John Bradshaw*

Mastering the Art of Making Money – *Joseph T.Riach*

Schindler's Ark – *Thomas Keneally*

Self Improvement Should Be Fun! – *Joseph T.Riach*

The Bible - *Various*

The Collected Works of Carl Jung – *Carl Jung*

The Complete Psychological Works of Sigmund Freud – *Sigmund Freud*

The Emperor's New Clothes – *Hans Christian Andersen*

The Simplest Sales Strategy – *Joseph T.Riach*

The Works of Lord Byron – *George Gordon Byron*

The Works of Mark Twain – *Mark Twain*

The Works of Robert 'Rabbie' Burns – *Robert Burns*

The Works of William Shakespear -   *William Shakespeare*

The Works of Winston Churchill – *Sir Winston Churchill*

Online

Author's Press Releases – *ibosocial.com/wakeup2wealth*

Author's Web Site – *www.tomriach.com*

Entertainment and Films

My Way - *Song written by Claude François and Jacques Revaux in 1967 as "Comme d'Habitude". English lyrics by Paul Anka. Famously recorded by Frank Sinatra*

Schindler's List - *Co-producer and director Steven Spielberg, writer Steven Zaillan based on the novel by Thomas Keneally. Academy Award Best Film 1994*

Quotes

"A song, a dance and a silly walk" - *Max Wall*

"Anyone with ambitions to be a politician ….. " - *Billy Connolly*

"Do not bear false testimony" - *the Bible*

"Give and ye shall receive ….. " - *the Bible*

"Look after yourself ….. " - *my Mum*

"Nothing in the world can take the place of persistence … " - *Ray Kroc*

"Paddy on the railway ….. " - *my Uncle Charlie, original unknown*

"Presentation!" - *Oskar Schindler*

"Religion was invented ….." - *Mark Twain*

"The best laid schemes o' mice an' men ….." - *Robert 'Rabbie' Burns*

" ….. the optimist sees the opportunity in every difficulty" – *Sir Winston Churchill*

"The steep, frowning glory of dark Lochnagar" - *Lord George Gordon Byron*

"There is no quiet place in the white man's cities" - *Chief Seattle*

"These must indeed be splendid clothes ….." - *Hans Christian Andersen*

"Whenever you find yourself on the side of the majority ….. " - *Mark Twain*

"You never know 'til a dead horse kicks you" - *my Uncle Charlie*

Sources of Inspiration

Hans Christian Andersen – *Author and playwright*

Harry Barclay – *Scottish farmer and businessman*

Brigitte Bardot – *Iconic French film star and animal rights activist*

Jeff Bezos - *Amazon.com founder and technology entrepreneur*

Richard Branson – *Millionaire entrepreneur and adventurer*

Sergey Brin – *Google co-founder*

Iain Bruce – *Lawyer and doctor of homeopathy*

Robert 'Rabbie' Burns – *Poet and national bard of Scotland*

Michael Caine – *Film star*

Sir Winston Churchill – *Politician and writer*

Billy Connolly – *Comedian and film actor*

Tom Cruise – *Film star*

Dance With The Wind – *Fictional creation of the author*

Erna Dewachter – *Gardener, independent thinker*

Clint Eastwood – *Film star and movie director*

Bill Gates – *Microsoft founder and business magnate*

Lulu Goodman – *Flower girl and events organiser*

Reverand MacIlwraith – *Church of Scotland minister*

Henry Moore – *Artist and sculptor*

Moses – *Biblical character, leader of the Jews*

My Mum

My Uncle Charlie – *Master baker, unwitting historian and philosopher*

Laurence Olivier – *Actor, movie star and director*

Larry Page – *Google co-founder*

Pablo Picasso - *Painter, sculptor, printmaker, ceramicist, stage designer, poet and playwright*

François Rodin – *Sculptor*

Oskar Schindler – *German industrialist*

Chief Seattle – *Suquamish and Duwamish chief (1786 - 1866)*

William Shakespeare – *Playwright*

Frank Sinatra – *Singer, film star and producer*

Carlos Slim – *Business magnate*

Ken 'Short' Smith – *Business manager*

Mark Twain – *Author, humourist, entrepreneur, publisher and lecturer*

Max Wall – *Comedian and actor*

Mark Zuckerberg – *Facebook.com, chairman and CEO*

Other References

Aberdeen – *Scotland's third city*

Aberdeen Grammar School – *One of oldest schools in UK, founded 1257*

Bavaria – *A federal state of Germany*

Bitcoin – *A type of digital currency*

Bordeaux – *Port city and wine capital in south west France*

Crypto Currency – *Virtual currency using cryptography security*

Cumbernauld – *Town in central Scotland*

John Deere & Company – *Agricultural, construction and heavy machinery manufacturer*

Flying Scotsman – *Famous British steam locomotive*

Georgian era - *period in British history, 1714 to circa 1830–37*

Glasgow – *Third largest British city*

Hornby Railways - *British model railway manufacturer*

Kendal Cake – *Glucose based mint confection popular among mountaineers and climbers*

Klondike – *Region in Yukon, northwest Canada famous for gold rush of 1896-99*

Lochnagar – *Mountain in Scotland*

London – *Capital city of United Kingdom*

Mallard – *Holder of world steam locomotive speed record*

Smartphone – *Electronic communication device*

St.Emilion – *Town and wine region in south west France*

Wake Up – *The author's leisure and learning breaks, personal mentoring and business guidance courses which he conducts in the sunny south of Portugal.* <u>*www.ibosocial.com/wakeup2wealth*</u>

You *can read all about Tom, his work and his latest publications at* <u>*www.tomriach.com*</u>

COPYRIGHT AND DISCLAIMER

Winning Big In Life And Business

Dare To Be Different And Own Your Own Future!

ISBN : 978-1798926628

author have used their best efforts in preparing this book, they make no representations or warranties with respect to the accuracy or completeness of the contents of this book and specifically disclaim any implied warranties of merchantability or fitness for a particular purpose. It is sold on the understanding that the publisher is not engaged in rendering professional services and neither the publisher nor the author shall be liable for damages arising herefrom. If professional advice or other expert assistance is required, the services of a competent professional should be sought. This manuscript relates only the personal experience of the author.

This manuscript relates only the personal experience of the author. Where reference is made to equity options, crypto currency, stocks and shares and trading in these products, it is made only as a factual account of real experience. This book is not recommending that you do or do not use any specific trading system and readers considering participating in equity option or crypto currency trading are strongly advised to seek proper professional advice from an accredited stockbroker or investment advisor. The past performance of shares, equity options and crypto currencies are not necessarily indicative of future performance and the price of shares, equity options and crypto currencies can go in the opposite direction to that expected. No liability is accepted by the author or publisher or their servants or agents for the use by any readers of the information contained herein in any circumstance connected with actual trading or otherwise. The author is not a stockbroker nor investment adviser in terms of the Financial Services Act 1986 or otherwise and this book does not give any specific investment advice, it is not asking for investment funds, it is not inviting readers or offering to invite readers into any investment agreement directly or indirectly. The book is not advising readers on the merits of shares, equity options or crypto currencies nor is it advertising them and it is not inviting readers to buy or sell, or not to buy or sell, shares, equity options or crypto currencies. Whilst all reasonable care has been taken to ensure that the information contained in this publication is accurate and not misleading at the time of publication, neither the author, nor the publisher nor their servants nor agents, is responsible for any errors or omissions contained in this publication which is published for information only and does not constitute, or claim to constitute, investment advice.